Standing On

Bended Knees

Randy M. Haynes (signature)

REV. DR. RANDY M. HAYNES

Standing On Bended Knees

"Real Talk for Real Men"
DEVOTIONAL

REV. DR. RANDY M. HAYNES

Standing On Bended Knees: "Real Talk for Real Men"
Devotional

Copyright © 2021 by Talk 2 The Text, LLC

Library of Congress Number – 2021909873 – Cataloging-in-Publication Data

Haynes, Randy,
Standing On Bended Knees
1. Spirituality. 2. Religion.

Printed in the United States of America
Dulles Publishing Company
44715 Prentice Drive #62
Ashburn, Virginia 20146

Acknowledgments

It's an expression that is perhaps often overused, but, nevertheless, it is a heartfelt truth for me. My wife, Lisa J. Haynes, who is the queen of my life, has been the wind beneath my wings for thirty-three years of marriage, plus some. Thank you, honey, for your relentless work on this book and for being the daughter of God. The inconvenient truth for me is that I might not quite be the son of God that I am if you were not the daughter of God that you are.

I also want to say a word about my son, Rev. Michael E. Haynes, II, a youth pastor and the proprietor of an exciting youth curriculum called "G-Shades." Son, from the early days after your conception, it has been my prayer that you'd grow up to be like a mighty oak. For sure, you are a qualitatively better man spiritually than I was at your age, and that fills me with exceeding contentment. May the distinct imprint of your ministry continue to be a blessing to the mission of the body of Christ to reach the world.

To my daughters—Gabrielle, Asha, Shekora, Diandra, Tiffany, Melinda, and Nicole - you are like sweet droplets that enrich the taste of my life. My prayer is that this book will further inspire and empower men to love gorgeous women like you even better. Never forget that women must be prepared to complement incoming male godly qualities with existing female godly qualities.

Lastly, one of my beloved sons in the ministry, Pastor Tony Ray Smith, has amassed quite a bit of experience in the area of writing and book publication. In fact, one of his books is on writing a book, *You Can Write a Book*, Dulles Publishing Co. Thank you, Tony, for your skills and for using them to place a watchful eye on my project with the objective that God would be glorified and kingdom men edified.

Introduction

"Trust in the Lord with all your heart, and lean not on your own understanding; but in all your ways acknowledge Him, and He shall direct your paths." (Proverbs 3:5-6).

Perhaps as far back as the 1940s, my dad, Rev. Dr. Michael E. Haynes, Sr., resolutely set that verse as the guiding beacon for his life. I want to dedicate this devotional book to him because he served as my best model for what robust and spiritual manhood looks like. Although my teen and young adult years were filled with both soaring spiritual tackles and miserable fumbles, I kept my dad's high and holy standards for living as a bar that I was determined to reach. Two things can be mutually true, so, while it's true that "knowing better means you're supposed to do better," the tasty, moist lick of sin hounded me like most young men, and I continue to regretfully gaze back at "the years the locusts have eaten." To be a real man surrendered to the mighty hand of God—and thereby gaining His provision, protection, power, and purpose—requires both a transformative discovery of who God really is and a dogged reach to bow to His majesty. My dad reeked with the undeniable scent of a real man. Even now, with an AARP card in my wallet and the benefits of spiritual maturity firmly shoved into my pockets, my best-reaching inner spiritual aspirations still whisper, "I wanna be like Mike."

This devotional book is structured to engage men for a full calendar year of fifty-two weeks. Most devotional guides I've encountered over the years are daily bites of thought. My hope is that after reading each weekly thought in this devotional book, men will spend the remainder of the week intentionally rereading and contemplating what's been written. I challenge men to look further into the broader scriptural context of each week's texts, possibly journaling, and even seizing opportunities to chat with other men about that week's reading and its accompanying thoughts. For sure, taking a full week to contemplatively chew on the thoughts offered in each weekly devotional will be a substantive weekly buffet. The content could also be adjusted and used for small men's groups in whatever way best suits a group's structure.

I want to insert a personal anecdotal note here. I am a Christian man but, because I also ascribe to a high degree of celebration for how God chose to specifically create me. I am also plumb pleased to say I am a Christian and a black man. Although I have had extensive experience ministering in white church venues for over forty years, I am a Christian black preacher with native roots in an inner city. Hence, some of my language and phrasings are influenced by my cultural anchoring and my specific individuality as a black preacher. Men tend to have little patience with cutie-pie articulation that reeks with a scent of cluelessness as to the challenges, struggles, allurements, and natural warrior heartbeats of real men who are trying to live out the gospel in the real world. Those who've sat under my ministry will tell you that I lean in the direction of "tell it like it is raw writing, teaching, and preaching." Given that my intended target here is real men and/or men who want to become real men, there may be spots in the reading where you might need to buckle up, put on your big boy underpants, and swallow hard.

I encourage sisters in the body of Christ to also finger through the pages of this devotional book in order to see what provocative challenges from the Word of God are being put to men. Of course, if you feel so led, I hope you'll make a copy available to the brothers, sons, husband, dad, nephews, neighbors, co-workers, and other men in your life who might not encounter it without a bit of feminine assistance. There will be many instances when sisters only need to flip the masculine reference to a feminine one for appropriate self-reflection and challenge, so, sisters, have at it!

Table of Contents

Acknowledgments...I

Introduction III

Table of Contents..VII

Week 1   A Sweet Hangover............................1

Week 2   Man on Top of Man.........................5

Week 3   Best Sex Ever 8

Week 4   Tippy-Toes 11

Week 5   How's Your Butt?...........................14

Week 6   Dirty Underpants..........................18

Week 7   Me Denying Me.............................21

Week 8   WHO?..26

Week 9   Practical, Not Just Technical...........30

Week 10   Vomit Between My Toes...............34

Week 11   Pleased but Puzzled....................38

Week 12   Morning Breath 43

Week 13   Tonguing Sin 46

Week 14   The Blocking Scent of Sin 49

Week 15   Five Responsibility Questions.......54

Week 16   GodIDon'tUnderstand 59

Week 17   It Can't Be Holy........................62

Week 18   Life Sucks? 65

Week 19 Moment of Impact 68

Week 20 Legs on Fish 72

Week 21 Be the Girl......76

Week 22 Free at Last......80

Week 23 Man Secrets......84

Week 24 Reading His Own News 89

Week 25 Scooby-Doo 93

Week 26 Expedite the Crash 97

Week 27 Man On Fire......102

Week 28 That BIG Butt......107

Week 29 What's Your Name?......111

Week 30 When God Ain't Godly......114

Week 31 Squirrel Butt......118

Week 32 Brother Delicious......121

Week 33 "Your Reach Should Exceed Your Grasp" ..124

Week 34 Boy in progress......127

Week 35 A Temporary God 130

Week 36 Lick It, Stick It, Hold It 134

Week 37 Dead Men's Shoes......137

Week 38 Chick Flicks 143

Week 39 Bitter Fork 151

Week 40 God's Daughter 155

Week 41 I Went Looking Again 159

Week 42 Too Fat to Fight 163

Week 43 A Casual Vacancy......167

Week 44 Sin Is my friend 171

Week 45 Marriage Hell/Hell of a Marriage 175

Week 46 I Don't Like Jesus 177

Week 47 The Humble Audacity of Me 181

Week 48 Unnecessarily Necessary? 184

Week 49 I Am What I'm Not 187

Week 50 When A Man Loves a Boy 190

Week 51 When a Man Loves a Man 194

Week 52 Nuggets From the Door Knock of Death ... 199

Week 53 Be Alive When You Die 206

Author 215

References 217

Week 1

A Sweet Hangover

Genesis 2:4–7

When God made man, He was clearly saying something about Himself and His creation of the world. I remain unconvinced, however, that we know and understand as much as we could. We can only imagine what God called upon within Himself to create and operationalize man. I love Genesis 2:7 and how it simply says, **"And the Lord God formed man of the dust of the ground, and breathed into his nostrils the breath of life; and man became a living being."** I love those simple yet profound words because they signal the instance in time when God gazed upon man and man gazed back at God. What a special moment in the pause of time it must have been! The earlier description (Genesis 1:26) only tells us that God did make man, but not how. An analytical look at Genesis 2:7 suggests a key component of God's creative work was preparation. Yes, God used what He made—dust—to make what He chose to create—man.

Most of us probably don't often consciously think about the fundamental connection between man and dirt. Yet our experiences of seeing life come to an end tells us that yes, eventually we will all some day close our eyes and return to the basics of our initial physiology—dirt.

Don't miss the preparatory work of God for the existence of man. The earth was first formed, and the rudiments of the environment were prepared to sustain man. Imagine the sweetness of Adam's first moments as he came to his consciousness of existence and drank in the presence of the One to whom he owed his existence. Imagine the first night of Adam's existence, perhaps after the extended creation had finally ended, and then imagine what flooded his soul as he experienced the sun's early dawn light the next day. The critical building blocks of our individual lives, which include the needed empowerment for our spiritual well-being, are set in motion by God. Our challenge is to run toward the plan, provision, and purpose of what He has prepared and not away from them. The psalmist, David, who knew what spiritual, physical, and emotional destitution were, nevertheless finally arrived at a place where he could say, "You (God) prepare a table before me . . . " (Psalm 23).

As I read Genesis 2:7, I can't help but notice that man did not develop into the intention of God until the preparation of God bridged to Adam's intimacy with God ("God breathed into his nostrils"). It was a pressing necessity—the breath of life— that gave man his initial life awakening. As we think about how we close each new night and begin each new day, let's be sure to consciously fight against the things in life that can easily distract us from the benefits of closing each new night with a God-consciousness and of beginning each new day with power meetings with God. As a man, that's exactly what I need from God. I need a regular infusion, metaphorically speaking, of intimate encounters where His breath blows on me and in me and revitalizes me in an intimate way for the bookends of each day. Some of you know what it's like to consume more alcohol at night than is wise, and you consequently wake up with a bad hangover. Or you engage in some other activity that closes a night in an unhealthy way that then bleeds into a regret-tinged morning. Bulking up on our knowledge of God and leaning into a daily life that begins and ends each new day with an intentional God-consciousness as a practice positions us to awaken each day with a "Sweet Hangover."

Week 2

Man on Top of Man

Genesis 2

God has stamped the need for a community into our spiritual DNA. Show me a man who stubbornly stands alone, largely closed off from hearing and considering the thoughts of others. I'll show you a deeply dysfunctional man who doesn't understand that God created us to thrive best in a community. God said about Adam, "It's not good for man to be alone." That was said because, in the early nice-to-meet-you dawn of creation, it became quite clear that the company of mere animals was not sufficient to buttress Adam's sense of connectivity and purpose.

You are a man, and your eyes gaze upon both bright darkness and dark darkness as you search for subtle threats to your emotional, mental, and physical well-being. Your shoulders are strong, and your chest protrudes like a fleshly, gleaming shield that's ready and able to handle the fiery darts of this worldly domain. The ripples and rumbles of your six-pack can withstand and survive the boom of unexpected incoming punches from life. In thirty to sixty seconds, your "manly package" can pick up on a frequency and then blast the hooks, locks, and moist chains off of any inviting sexual nest. Then you can be asleep seven minutes after the initial action was initiated. Your legs are remarkable mechanical pillars of endurance, and your feet have taken you to and from environmental extremes from inhospitable jungles of war to the ivory corridors of academia. You are da man!!! But alas, not only are you a man, but it should also be duly noted that in the end—even if you allow the exaggerations—you are just a man.

Jesus could have come to earth and could have done His "thang" as a singular trumpet, blowing the call and invitation to salvation, but He didn't. He took the time to recruit other men to walk with Him, hang out with Him, recreate with Him, strategize with Him, build a friendship with Him, take on hard times with Him, and carry forth the truth of the gospel for Him.

Whether you've been a Green Beret or a part of some other elite testosterone-laden group, let's remind ourselves that God desires us to function in a community. By way of a man's testimony, one of the most satisfying venues a man can find in Christian circles is a good men's group. When such a group is led well and organized well, it's an example of where men can safely take their "stuff" and get wisdom, practical and personal support, and where they can value accountability. You may have moments of aloneness and loneliness, and it might even suit God's purposes for you to visit with one or both, but it's critically important for you to know you were not created to live there. We are best when we close ranks and get men together with men.

Week 3

Best Sex Ever

Genesis 2:4–25; Psalm 127:4–5

Sometimes I can't stand Adam! Think about how pretty his setup was because it was absolutely pristine and privileged! He had a healthy soul in a healthy body connected to a perfect relationship with a perfect woman!! Please, somebody, wipe the drool from the corners of my mouth because this brother had it going on. Admittedly, it's hard for us to fully appreciate that because all we've ever known is the cotton field of masculine imperfection. We often quietly face the natural limitations of our physical selves, even as we falsely brag about our male prowess and what we've delivered in our reigning moments of "Daddy is in the house" exploits! But Adam had no such issues. We strain our brains to comprehend our women's complexities as we wipe the crap off of our shoes that we desperately tried not to step in. But alas, we did, and all hell was unleashed on us because, in the end, we proved ourselves yet again clueless. Adam had no such issues.

You see, before the fall, Adam perfectly appreciated the love of intimacy, and he enjoyed the intimacy achieved thru perfect loving. Adam, before the fall, is my hero because he could carry piles of wood through the garden, get sweaty, and fifteen seconds later still carry Eve to the chamber of love. His physiology presumably exceeded the energy lull of our current sin-degenerative bodies. He could say whatever he chose to say because his mind, will, attitude, perspectives, and values were perfectly calibrated to fall with ease and sweetness into the delicious and lickable ears of Eve. He didn't even have to erase a week off of the monthly calendar because the possibility of a sexual encounter was a complete "no-go" that week. No, Adam did not have such issues. When God told Adam and Eve to be "fruitful and multiply," I can only imagine that Adam ramped that into fifth gear. He put his back into it, closed his eyes, and sweetly groaned a line from a Luther Vandross song. The applause from watchful forest creatures could be heard from all directions. That, my brothers, was the wondrous gift of God, and Adam has been the only man to know what that was like in its perfect form. Don't weep too heavily, though, for God has preserved a form of "bing, bam, boom" that's still marvelous although no longer perfect.

Be sure to never forget that God does things and gives all things with intention. The Divine intention is for us to enjoy the gift in the context of marriage (Hebrews 13:4). Many of us who faltered will tell you if you're single, be sure to wrap your "package" in spiritual ice and let it "idle" until God brings you to the buffet-rich garden of marriage. For those who are married, in the spirit of Adam, let's take care of our bedroom business and honor the daughter of God before, during, and after we seek to engage in the best (post-Adam) sex ever.

Week 4

Tippy–Toes

Genesis 3

In Genesis 3, God spotted Adam's "raggedy butt" tiptoeing through the underbrush of the garden forest (hiding). Yeah, Adam had triggered an unpleasant need to be confronted by God because he had been an affront to God. Look, can you see him? Even if you can't see him, I can see him quite clearly, and the reason I can see him is because I can easily see myself in him! I can see myself stupidly ducking and dodging under branches and dumbly trying to escape the peering, transcendent eyes of Father God. I can see my slumped shoulders carrying the moisture of fresh sin that's dancing upon and dripping from my sin-burdened shoulders. I can see the dark smoky clouds of carnal thought seeping and escaping from the tunnels of my ears. I'm catching glimpses of the red spots on my eyes that stem from my visual fixation on multiple things that are unholy. I can see a faint stained imprint of female-shaped buttocks on the center of the palms of my hands, and they got there because I often grabbed and held them with all my Mandingo might, even though they weren't mine to grab. I can see kernels of vain thought popping from the center of my brain because I previously bought into the jacked-up delusion that I was the master of my destiny.

Despite the thick bushels of sin that separated me from my better self, I can hear the voice of my feet telling stories about places I should not have gone. Between the camouflage of multi-colored leaves, I'm able to catch glimpses of my lips as they pucker from the sad and sour taste of spoken words that didn't matter and empty untruths that didn't satisfy. As I watch myself from several yards away, I know that I'm on my tippy-toes (as I wear Adam's fleshly robe) because I think I'm getting away with something. It's still not altogether clear to me that whatever man does in the dark shall someday come to light (Luke 12:2-3).

You see, as I watch myself tiptoeing in that garden, it occurs to me that what I don't yet know is that God's impending confrontation of me and declaration that I've affronted His holiness is actually an act of love on His part. You see, it's a privilege to have the sovereign God of the universe care enough about you to come and get you to keep the devil from eternally having you.

Men, as Adam tiptoed and weaved his way between the trees hoping to encounter the conspiratorial cover of tall grass, his unfamiliar new desire to not be seen by God darkened his soul, and his behavior was a witness against him. Herein lies a truth that we should not want to be like Adam. Instead of mirroring the dumb tiptoeing of Adam in our own lives, let's instead determine to stomp the ground in recognition that evil exists and it's not out for our good. Let's stomp the ground with the type of repentance that causes us to run toward the hug of forgiveness. Let's stomp the ground and declare a partnership with God to uphold the righteousness of God. Let's stomp the ground to say, here I stand, and for God, I shall die.

Week 5

How's Your Butt?

Genesis 3

You may have noticed that I've pulled to the side of the road, and I've parked on the street that intersects where Adam was confronted by God because of His affront to God. I am hanging around on this street because if we as men don't clearly view the issues of sin, God's heart, and God's nonnegotiable requirements, we're doomed to drive in circles for the remainder of our lives. I don't think anybody will get punched in heaven, but Adam might want to punch me in the face when I corner him to ask intrusive questions about what he was thinking, doing, hoping, plotting, and praying for after the fall. While I'm sure my current desire will have no place in the reality of heaven, I really do want to crawl retrospectively into the dark cavity of his freshly minted sin predicament so that I can understand the raw concept of original sin in the immediate context of his post-sin environment. I should quickly admit that I have some nerve even thinking such a thing because I wouldn't want others retrospectively searching my past dark cavities!

.

It has been said, "If you want peace, prepare for war." In a spiritual context, that is also absolutely true! We cuddle Satan, hug Satan, talk politely to Satan, tolerate his incessant verbiage, hang out with him, and make excuses for dancing with him. And what does he do?

- He guts our strength by habitually placing before us more than we should take on.
- He steps in and devastates our families when we take our eyes off of home plate by making them secondary and tertiary.
- He wrecks our finances because we fail to see it's not our money.
- He infiltrates our churches, in part because men oftentimes don't actively step up and hold up the pastor's arms which contributes to a weaker corporate body.
- He convinces us that the impact of an unauthorized booty call lasts only as long as the call.
- He waters down the preacher's sermons by convincing us that truth is subjective.

- He poisons our tongues by surrounding us with influential friends who have poisonous tongues.

- He sets us up to think that privacy of thought can't be harmful if kept private, and Satan thereby slowly tries to steer our feet into the deep waters of moral compromise because he knows where the natural flow of the current can take us!

So, yeah, since Adam was the first fresh (man) meat that Satan (via the serpent's instrument) went after, I'd love to hear the details of how he handled himself after the fall even though, again, it's not my business. In the meantime, back here at the "Haynes ranch," I know I need to sharpen my steel-plated spiritual cowboy boots further because the devil is not intimidated by my ecclesiastical title and it's often wartime! I've got a soul to guard. I've got a wife counting on me to lead spiritually and not just talk a good talk. I've got offspring who are counting on me to be what I say I am. I've got friends who look to me to stand up, show up, and hold up the blood-stained banner. I've got baby Christians who are looking to follow me as I follow Christ. I've got a Christ community that's counting on me not to embarrass our God nor embarrass them. Yeah, when lulls in demonic attack occur, I've got to use those moments to again "Prepare for War." And by the way, serious soldiers understand that a man doesn't simply walk out on a battlefield without proper preparation. Let me say this straight: If you're routinely getting your "head and butt" kicked and handed back to you, it's because you're not adequately prepared for war! If you don't regularly make time for Bible study, your butt is grass. If you don't routinely reach for the practice of holiness in your private life, your butt is grass. If you don't position yourself for kingdom service in Christ's church, your butt is grass. If you don't have a daily prayer life, your butt is grass! So, let me ask, "How's your butt?"

Week 6

Dirty Underpants

Genesis 3

Frequently, one plus one doesn't quite equal two in the same way in God's mind as it does in our minds. In the economy of our human intellectual and emotional standard for justice, a wrong is supposed to be measurably met by a correction or a corrective punishment. I recently heard a preacher say something that was dead on. He said, "There is no such thing as a sin that doesn't harm somebody." While God knows that's true, the sometimes and additionally uncomfortable and puzzling truth is that God does not play "life chess" with us. Often time, He doesn't immediately respond, in kind, to a move we've made or not made. His transcendence allows Him to "act" out His will whether we're measurably able to discern His action or not. At times, it will be within His purpose for us to know He has "acted." At other times, it will not suit His divine purpose for us to have a clue what He will do, when He will do it, why He will do it, and/or even if it's already done.

Here I go again. I'd love to step back in time and interview Adam at the "one year living in sin" anniversary mark. Sin and its specific motivations and the rippling impacts behind it can be a bit layered. I don't know it for a fact, but I'm suspicious that Adam did not have a theologically tight understanding of the broader ramifications of the fall. Yes, he knew what he (and his Halle Berry look-alike boo) did was wrong because he had to stand before God and accept the consequences. Still, he likely did not understand the devastating results of his action and how it actually shifted the earth's spiritual tilt for all of humanity.

If I were able to step back into time and give Adam some counsel based on the extended riverbank of sin that has my name embroidered along the weed-filled grassy knoll of life, I'd start with an admission and then offer two words of counsel.

Admission: Adam, let me say that the basis of my counsel is not a mastery of righteousness in my life but, instead, I speak as one man who for a long time paid rent to sin, bought it food, burped it, and lovingly tucked it in at night.

Counsel One: Adam, don't let your knowledge that "God loves" cause you to bet that sin doesn't matter. You see, Adam, God loves you, but He doesn't love your dirty underpants, so knock off the proactive decisions to soil them and also keep an eye on generational sin-bends as you begin parenting.

Counsel Two: Every attempt you make to lead your woman, your kids, or anyone or anything else will spiritually fail if you don't understand that you must allow the Holy Spirit to teach you to first lead yourself.

Real men, too often we wait on our women, our mothers, unexpected storms, or the preacher to "check our underpants!" With the Holy Spirit as your guide, regularly unzip your spiritual trousers, drop 'em, and take a peek.

Week 7

Me Denying Me

Genesis 3

Will a man's very soul testify against him? That is the question that fundamentally comes to mind as I continue to crawl around in the shadowy tunnel with my good friend, Adam. In most ways, I suspect he and I, and he and you, and you and I are more similar than we know. Why? Because humanity is what it is, and fundamentals tend to be fundamental no matter the generation, ethnicity, culture, or orientation. I'm in search of the answer to the following two questions for Adam and, frankly, also for me: "What are the things I must do and, and what are the things I must not do?

As Adam moved about in his "birthday suit," hiding from the God who made him, I can only imagine the dizzying swirl of self-denial that coursed through his new sinful veins. At that moment, God ignored Adam's mentally paralyzing new embarrassment and confronted him face to face in the cool of the garden day because there were known answers that needed to be matched to questions. Although God knew the answers, the questions were asked nonetheless: "Adam, where art thou? Adam who told you that you were naked? Adam, have you eaten from the tree I told you not to eat from?"

I'm going to admit something here, and I'm asking that you tell nobody because it's my secret? Each of God's questions to Adam can be asked of me right now. I'll put my name in there, but you know whose name you're supposed to put in there:

1. "Haynes, where art thou?" Yeah, that question can be put to me by God because I'm still not completely and consistently where I'm supposed to be by connecting intimately with the Lord God in my head and heart. In Scripture and in our individual lives, the penetrating questions of God—including questions regarding our location—should attract our attention as our feet move to places they ought not to be. The "where art thou" question has even more unsettling implications when applied outside of the inquiry of a specific geographical location.

Our values, habits, and ability to actually recognize God's voice, show thoughtful care for God's creation, exhibit honor for mother and father, practice sensible care of our bodies as temples of God, routinely treat our spouses with dignity, and more, are all areas where God's question to Adam can be directed to us.

2. "Haynes, who told you that you were naked?" Again, if I'm experiencing discomfort with God's company and with what God is actually comfortable with, something is very wrong. You see, there are times when we recoil from that which God takes pleasure in such as unfettered kindness, unconditional love, unguarded forgiveness of others, a willingness to be vulnerable, and even the importance of a well-placed and sincere apology. In principle, that presses my face against the windowpane of life because, time and time again, I can think of instances when my comfort or discomfort stood opposite to God's. For sure, God wants us to see and accept our realities based on His view of things and that includes acknowledging that we've had an unauthorized dance with sin.

God's question to Adam was not intended to deny his nakedness. Rather, God was asking Adam to recognize that his slime-ball, bush hiding behavior was not normal.

3. "Haynes, have you eaten from the tree I told you not to eat from?" The critical issue here is disobedience. Adam, like a punk, quickly pointed to Eve, and Eve quickly pointed to the serpent. Time and time again, I must admit that I've been disobedient. Likewise, my instinct has often been to somehow justify the disobedience by highlighting either the leadership, partnership, and/or followers who willingly went along with me. For me, I'm sometimes disobedient—not as much because I don't move after hearing God say to move—but, rather, disobedient because I take my sweet time moving because I don't approve of God's timing.

An example would be, I'm disobedient when I show only basic passing courtesies to someone when God says to show big demonstrable love. As men, there are times when sin restfully abides with us—not because a thought becomes actionable—

but, rather, because the thought enjoys passive, peaceful existence in our heads. For many of us, the deeper and broader application of God's question ("Have you eaten from the tree . . .") requires an earnest analysis of our individuality as we live before the One true God.

God created you and me in His image. As a Christian man, if I deny my redeemed basic God-implanted image, that's me also denying me.

Week 8

WHO?

Genesis 3

I didn't mention it before, but this might be my favorite line in Adam's entire saga: "Who told you that you were naked?" (Genesis 3:11). I love that question from God because it's the first time God is recorded asking a question in response to what a man has said and beneath the question lies an awakening. You see, when a man does what God has commanded, does it the way God has commanded, does it when God commands, does it for the reason God commands, there will be little need for God to ask a question. And, by the way, the question was not actually for God's informational purposes. Rather, it was a rhetorical question that was intent on leading Adam down the spiritual street of reconciliation. Yeah, there were things Adam should not have known (the taste of the forbidden fruit), and the fact that he knew its taste says that he had inappropriately been in connectivity with a force (the serpent) who had exposed Eve, and then him, to something he had no business knowing (the taste of the forbidden fruit). You see, as a man, I have a choice—just like Adam. I can walk down certain streets of "experimental experience" to verify the taste of stuff I've heard about or witnessed from a distance. Or, I can choose to believe the ravages of sin as its hollow voice screams from the shredded lives of others. Even better and smarter, I can do what Adam had an opportunity to do in person, which was to believe God when He said, "You would do well not to taste that. I know it looks good. I know you can well imagine how delectable its caress would be. I know you're curious about its potency and the possible delight of being left flat on your back grinning from the raging mix of an orgasmic explosion and stolen yum-yum. I know you suspect it might bolster your reputation among other men. I know you're convinced you'll be able to play it in a balanced, controlled way because you think it will want you more than you want it. I know it'll position you in the marketplace to enjoy prestige, power, and influence like never before."

You see, men, the tragedy lies beneath God's "who" question because for God to ask "who" meant that someone other than Himself had momentarily gained use of the microphone and had spoken an alternative into Adam and Eve's tastebuds.

I look at me, and I look at you, and I dare to ask the question, "Who?" Who told me/you that we could politely ignore the summons of God to be more than a church attendee and not eventually tick God off? Who told me/you that we could get away with living inside our heads and entertaining thoughts that don't honor God and think we're free and in the clear? Who told me/you that kingdom involvement belongs at the bottom of our priority list? Who told me/you that we're doing the preacher a favor when we show up on Sunday morning? Who told me/you that our work life is totally separate from who we are in our church life? Who told me/you that a quick "thrusting panty raid" of the "church hottie" is reasonably harmless if nobody finds out? Who told me/you that it's proper to listen to what our wives say even ahead of what God says? Who authorized me/you to casually tolerate the lesser version of ourselves simply because it's still enough to impress the little church people? Who told me/you that our intellectual powers of reason could be safely placed ahead of God's declarations? Who told me/you that our politics has permission to further disenfranchise poor people? Who told me/you that how we treat our wives has nothing to do with the Lordship of Jesus Christ? Who told me/you that we are the ultimate masters of our personal business when it comes to choices over how we use our dollars? Who told me/you that our biblical illiteracy is just fine as long as the pastor is biblically literate? If Adam had wisely paused to ask WHO was behind the offer of the fruit, human existence wouldn't be groaning beneath the weight of its dire condition. Who?

Week 9

Practical, Not Just Technical

Genesis 3

Have you ever witnessed family blood relationships that can only be described as technical? Most of us probably have at least one blood relationship that, if the raw truth be told, our feelings, care, and connections with that person are no more intimate than the servers we regularly encounter at Starbucks. Even after Adam did God wrong (Genesis 3), God continued to be his God and not just in a technical way but in practical ways. My dad often offered the following as his simple definition of what a Christian is: "A Christian is a person who has accepted Jesus Christ as Lord and Savior." After accepting Jesus as your Lord and Savior, if you pivot back to carnality as your norm, I'd contend you're living in a situation where God is only technically your God. He is not your God in a practical sin-freeing way and not in a practical way where He's called upon to direct the movement and contours of your life. And I've got news for you—it pains Father God to be your God just in a technical sense. You see, the institutional church does a disservice when it leaves the unspoken impression that God's place is in the hallowed halls of worship. In practical nitty-gritty ways, God wants to intimately intersect with a man in the church, in a man's house, in the White House, the schoolhouse, the crack house, and, yep, even in a whorehouse because there is no place where His love won't come and get you.

God reinforced His intimate and practical interests in the daily affairs of Adam's life, and we see it in what He said to Adam and what He did for Adam when He addressed Adam's sin. Yes, the practical hand of God was displayed in at least three ways.

First: **God affirmed the rightness of Adam's sexual masculinity**. Yeah, Adam must have stood by in amazement as he listened to his God tell his woman that even though she would now bear children in excruciating pain, she was still going to have a desire to creep up on Adam, "Drop it like it's hot and put it on him, again and again!" Can you say, "practical?"

Second: God affirmed Adam's masculine leadership. Even though Adam had deeply offended God by that one sin of disobedience, God still affirmed Adam's right to rule over the environment as well as take the lead role in his household. You see, God had built Adam a certain way, and He was practical in how He chose to affirm Adam's ongoing existence and masculine design even in his fallen state. Can you say, "practical?"

Third: God affirmed Adam's masculinity as a provider. A man must eat, and his family must eat. So, once again, God was very practical in how he dealt with Adam. Although it was new to Adam, he was assured he'd be able to use his God-given skill set to provide food for himself and his family, although it would be labor-intensive. A man who lacks the will to work is a substantial problem. Even though we now live in a very different culture wherein women often also work, it's fair to still underscore that God sowed an appropriate capacity and desire in Adam's heart to be a man who worked. Can you say, "practical?"

The songwriter said, "Our God is an awesome God." Know this as well, Our God is also a practical God.

Week 10

Vomit Between My Toes

Genesis 3

When Adam sinned, the heavy, steel blanket of sin lay across his head, heart, and soul. The harsh indicting words of God (Genesis 3:17–19) burst all around him but, amidst the cascade of divine verbal declarations came **liberation and mercy**. Yes, liberation and mercy lay beneath the almost overlooked words, "Till you return to the ground." Yep, God was referring to the fact that Adam would someday die. You see, it's important to look beyond the cloudy veil of human sight that almost always focuses our lives on the here and now. With His words, God signaled a realization that Adam himself had not yet come to grips with the reality that when you truly desire to live for God, sin will always attempt to circle, stab, and drain you of divinity. Yes, Adam didn't understand it, but if God had allowed him to live forever, it would have become grievously tiring to wrestle in the garbage bin of sin forever. In our current life span, we have perhaps seventy to ninety years on average to learn how to push away from the human pull of selfishness and lean toward God's expression of love. We have seventy to ninety years of challenges to speak the truth when it's easier to tell a lie. And we have seventy to ninety years of challenge for redirecting a penis GPS system that often stubbornly wants to have a mind of its own—most especially in the critical foundation laying younger years.

I have been liberated from actual enslavement to sin, but even yet, I sometimes get tired of the fight to submit to the powerful thrust of the Holy Ghost, and there are moments when I'd like to be french kissed by sin. Upon the first occasion of his sin encounter, Adam disobeyed God, which left him in a dire, spiritually sickened state. Along with Adam and me, you are a spiritually sick man in the sense that you and we have not yet crossed over into eternity, where we'll experience a fully new dimension of life without the wilder beast of sin crouching at our front doors. Until that day comes, let's continue to push to think, talk, behave, and serve God like we really are tired of being sickened by sin. In the text, the consequences of sin were starkly laid out for Adam, and they were punctuated by additional new and startling information, which was that he was now someday going to die. As was the case for Adam, it's incumbent upon men of God to think soberly about the quality of how we shall live before we die.

I think I'm right when I say almost nobody desires to be literally vomited on. Yet, spiritually speaking, we frequently tolerate not just our own vomit. We also tolerate others who routinely negatively impact us with their vomit. If a man signals a desire to engage with you as a man, romantically, and you choose to justify that type of engagement, check your toes (Romans 1). If you're idolizing an object, a system, or a person in place of God, check your toes (Romans 1). If your wife has convinced you there is no God-assigned distinction between a man and a woman, check your toes (Ephesians 5). If modernity and/or the children you're raising have pushed you to believe that it's OK for them to ignore your authority as a parent, check your toes (Ephesians 6). If you're on your way to thinking you should simply believe in yourself, and life is ultimately inconsequential because physical death is the end; check your toes (Revelation 19-20).

God showed Adam how nauseating the smelly spillage of sin can be, how its impact manages to quickly resonate in us and around us, and that it's never for our destined good. Adam must have been shell-shocked because he actually had two indisputable truths dropped on him, like two Tomahawk Missiles: 1) Sin in life can have real-time consequences, and 2) Yep, you're gonna die. The question for Adam, you, and me is, "Before we die, what will be our depth of toleration for the vomit of sin between our toes?"

Week 11

Pleased but Puzzled

Genesis 3; 2 Corinthians 5

When I was young, there was a period when I enjoyed the popular TV show, *I Love Lucy*. Lucy was married to a Cuban fellow named Ricky Ricardo and, although Ricky loved Lucy, he was often puzzled by her. In the end, however, he always admired the goodness of her heart and knew she always had his best interests in mind. He would often say, "Lucy, you've got some 'splainin' to do." His thick Cuban accent kept him from clearly annunciating the full word, "explaining." You know, I've got a feeling that Adam had many, many Ricky Ricardo moments because God, after all, is beyond the full comprehension of human beings. Although He is a communicator, He quite clearly has no sense of obligation to fully explain Himself to us—whether He's engineering an addition or a subtraction in our lives. It would be easy to slip into a litany of pain puzzlements that must have knocked Adam off-balance frequently, but I'm increasingly fascinated by the good stuff that must also have left Adam puzzled by the enigmatic nature of God.

Most certainly, Adam must have frequently opened his eyes every morning as the warm sunlight gently kissed his face and smiled. He greedily man-gazed at the incredible feminine creature lying beside him, who was still a wonder to behold despite her sin-bend. I don't know about you, but I'm struck by the fact that nowhere in the biblical text do we witness God verbally telling Adam that He loved him. I'll rely on someone more brilliant than I to do some deep-sea diving regarding that observation. Yet, as one example, His love was supremely evident by the seizure-inducing female gift He allowed Adam to have at his side. That gift kept on giving and must have puzzled Adam even as he grinned with his happy teeth. If you're a married man, I hope your individual attestation is similar to mine in the way of my profound realization that God has gifted me with one of his precious daughters as my soul mate. Just recently, unknown to her, I watched her as she moved about the kitchen. Beyond the multiple aspects of her physiology, such as the delicate movement of her feminine wrists or the swan-like elongation of her kissable neck, I momentarily settled into the thought of her relentless caretaking, intentional thought, and strategic planning. It is all directly rooted in her ceaseless drive to situate our home base for comfort and care, which means it's a place of lovely respite and restoration. Time and time again, she'll be busy on her laptop, and while most of the time I don't know what she's specifically doing, I'm certain that much of the time it has something to do directly or indirectly with the management of our lives. Can you say puzzled by God's good gifting?

Adam's puzzlement, of course, extended beyond the gift of Eve, for he also continued to enjoy the puzzlement of a future legacy. You see, he personally didn't cooperate with God's initial plan for him to have no legacy to leave behind because he was arguably not originally built to die. God also allowed him in other ways to have a legacy because of the birth of children. Lastly, I want to mention that God puzzled Adam by repeatedly extending the power of forgiveness. Yeah, Adam was now a sinner, and guess what sinners do? But yet, God used His loving fresh touch and refused the creeping "nudge of justice" that wanted to whack Adam and leave him swimming with the fish.

Now, what about you? Are you puzzled by the God who has given you that incredible woman you're dating, engaged to, or married to, and do you understand that it may be true that you don't deserve her? If she is no longer the type of woman who adds some sizzle to the bacon of life, do you understand that God can still alter and refresh a trajectory of love? Are you puzzled by the goodness of God when you reflect back on the roads of life He steered you away from? Are you puzzled by how God has positioned you to have a legacy, and do you understand that your "not so long-ago stupidity" could have canceled the possibility of a positive legacy? Are you tucking the amazing display and power of God's forgiveness in your shirt pockets and keeping them close because you understand how much that frees you and helps you to look like Jesus?

When a guilty-as-charged criminal stands before a judge, he doesn't expect to be lavished with good gifts. Yet, God has declared guilty men to be not guilty when they have accepted Jesus Christ as Lord and Savior, and then He lavishes us with other gifts. Are you puzzled?

Week 12

Morning Breath

Genesis 3

OK, I admit it. I am so, so nosy regarding information that the text declines to tell us. I am fascinated by questions regarding the nature, tone, and texture of Adam and Eve's relationship—both pre-fall and post-fall—but, most especially, post-fall. You see, I understand how a man handles the realities of an imperfect woman, but how does a man handle the realities of an imperfect woman after having first experienced her being perfect? Once again, I'm amused as I envision Adam in the future trying to tactfully avoid me in heaven as I pursue him for a one-on-one question and answer session.

I'm obviously not exactly sure of this, but I suspect I'm right when I say Adam will probably say something like the following after I corner him, twist his arm, and force him to talk about his long-ago daily dealings with his newly-minted, imperfect woman.

(In my sanctified imagination, Adam speaks)

"First, I took the time to recognize and appropriately mourn her loss—not just her loss of a perfect husband but also the loss of her front-row view of perfect leadership, perfect fatherhood, and the joy of watching her perfect man interact in harmony with her perfect God. Yes, I was actually heartbroken that she would never again experience the sweet epitome of man care and the perfection of male-female heart alignment. Nor would she experience the unfettered, balanced mixture of heart-soul-mind-body physical intimacy that lasts for as long as needed and as brief as desired. So yeah, Haynes, if you must know, I started my post-sin days with a part of me in a place of deep regret and mourning.

"Second, I had to free myself from could of, would of, should of thinking as it relates to what I as a man wished that she was, yet again. Yes, I learned to love and respect the woman who could be versus the woman she could never be again. It was hard at first but, once I reconciled myself to my new reality, I accepted her and even saw her new blemishes of sin in the same way that I saw blemishes on a beautiful stone. While I wasn't initially accustomed to stones in creation with imperfect markings, chips, and ragged edges, I've come to embrace their overall beauty and how they still hold their core design, as does she."

"Third, I learned to give thanks for the fact that although we as a couple could never be perfectly in line with the original intentionality of God, I could be thankful that even sin was unable to block our recognition of ourselves. We continued to exist as us, although as a lesser us. As we aged and our once firm, perfect bodies turned into apparent imperfect, aching, hard of hearing, wrinkled, weaker bodies, it only reminded us that God had created us with an eternal soul. He designed us so that one day we would leave earth's decay, and nothing will be able to separate us from loving one another or from the love of God."

Real men, I implore all of us as imperfect men to take a new look at the imperfect women that our perfect God has placed in our imperfect lives. Our imperfect relationships stand in the shadow of the perfect Christ who has taken the imperfect church to be His bride.

Week 13

Tonguing Sin

Genesis 3

Webster defines the word, "then" in the following way: "At that time. Soon after that. Next. In addition. Consequently."[i] Genesis 3:6 reports on the moments that Eve enjoyed munching on the forbidden fruit, and it also signals that she gave to Adam, and he ate." Verse 7 (in the NAS) starts with the word, "then." "Then the eyes of both of them were opened, and they knew . . ." [ii]

We can't be sure of the quantitative elapse of time between verse 7 and what verse 8 describes as them hearing God as He came into the garden. So, what I want to know from Adam is—as the leader of his relationship— what was going through his head and heart in the moments that fell between verse 7 and verse 8. That is to say, what does a man experience between the heaving moist doggish laps of sin and his personal encounter with Father-God?

Actually, I should stop "faking the funk" because I have at least three good ideas about what a man experiences between tonguing sin so deeply that he licks the paint off its walls and when God shows up and looks him in his nearly dead eyes.

Option One: The man slips, slides, and slinks beneath the dishonest covers of human stupidity. When a man does that, he cheats himself of a quick pardon and, therefore, further stiffens his dumb resolve to act dumb in the presence of the supreme, intelligent Creator God of the universe. I, for one, have been there.

Option Two: The man pretty quickly offers a rhetorical confession but fails to fully digest the wider implications of why his action is offensive to his Holy God. That, of course, means he'll soon be sitting once again in the smelly, soiled, soft, and messy diaper of manly proclivities. For you see, when you don't earnestly reach to understand God and let Him empower you to resist the lure of frequent man mess, it almost assuredly will repeatedly conquer you. I, for one, have been there.

Option Three: The man confesses from the depth of his soul and repentantly stands raw, naked, and undone before his heavenly Daddy. But he also stands ready to accept possible reverberations. That man also understands that even if negative reverberations are not visibly measurable by human perception, he's still sorrowful for having let his Father-God down. I, for one, have been there.

Can you figure out which description most closely fits Adam in his moment? Can you determine which description most closely fits you after your dances with sin?

Week 14

The Blocking Scent of Sin

Genesis 3:2; 2 Peter 2:19

A devotional thought from Dr. Charles Swindoll got me thinking about what Adam "found God to be and what he found God not to be." Prior to the fall, heaven and earth and all existing relationships—except the devil and his demonic imps—were in perfect alignment, and Adam understood that God was not a "heavenly bellboy" who was there for his "beck and call." In Dr. Swindoll's words, "He doesn't exist to make us happy. We exist to bring Him glory."[iii] The Gen 3:2 text signals a recognition of the divine standard, which involved the fragrant beauty of obedience.

Many, many years ago, I had the unfortunate experience of being present when first responders broke down a front door and discovered a dead body. The blast of putrid odor was like nothing I've ever experienced, and it was virtually disorienting for a few minutes. Post fall, sin's nasty armpit continued its putrid effort to infect Adam's habits, values, heart, soul, and mind. I know that because the Word signals that sin always likes to create a master-slave dynamic and, additionally, I've had a lot of real-life experience sniffing that armpit. Rather than trying to get you to deny God, a sinister trick of the "enemy" is to sometimes simply introduce sights, sounds and smells to cloud your focus. He doesn't need you to not believe in God. He simply needs to **minimize** you by influencing you to be a cloudy, unfocused believer in God. Additionally, sin's sponsor—the devil—doesn't have to try to fully destroy you because he may well settle on successfully using you.

Being caught under the armpit of sin and being overrun by its influential smell can cloud a man's mind regarding what God is and what God is not. Learning "what God is and what God is not" means we need to live with well-calibrated expectations of God, and that keeps us from nearly drowning in the pool of misdirected expectations of God. Shame on preachers who tout a gospel that leads people to believe that their happiness is of chief concern to God. God is chiefly concerned with His glory, not our happiness. In fact, it's in our struggles where we often meet Him deeply and grow substantively. After the fall, Adam must have quickly learned to see God through the sweat that gathered on his manly face and the tears that slid down his leathery cheeks. In his early creation context, who knows what specific environmental sights, sounds, and smells routinely emanated from the armpit of sin and threatened to cloud his understanding of his God. He, like us, was a man, so we can probably guess in principle how he had to fight past the cloudy scent of sin and routinely remind himself of a few things:

1. God does not owe us a blessed thing. All good gifts are exactly that, gifts. On top of that, whatever He righteously gives, He is likewise right if He chooses to take it away.

2. Real Men push to love God, serve God, spend time thinking about God, submit to God, tell others about God and feel no need to apologize that they're full of God.

3. Whatever God places in your hand, God expects you to properly care for it and properly manage it—such as a woman, spiritual gifting,

children, finances, leadership, influence, material things, ministry, knowledge, and wisdom.

4.   Like a good father, God's love for us is never-ending, but that does not mean He won't "kick the snot out of us" when we stubbornly abuse his forgiveness and love.

5.   God's divine intelligence exceeds the stupid human games we emotionally and psychologically play with one another. Even when humans swallow our crap and fail to notice how slick and manipulative we can be, God is always standing around the corner, awaiting our dumb arrival.

6.   For His own sovereign purpose, He chooses not to show Himself in physical ways that human eyes can easily perceive. He does wonderfully place men and women who represent Him in our paths, and it's up to us to value them and learn from them.

7.   He's given us multiple routes of communication with Him—the soul/spirit and the mind—and

the mouth can be involved or not involved, but in the end, it's up to us to reach back across the expanse to speak to His waiting ear.

Men, let's not allow the alluring and distracting scent of sin to block the clarity of our God, who wants us to see Him more clearly and love Him more dearly.

Week 15

Five Responsibility Questions

Genesis 3:12–16

Adam blamed Eve, Eve blamed the serpent, and the serpent wisely kept his mouth shut because God was about to pistol-whip him. It's interesting to me that God didn't immediately swat their verbal drool out of the air as it dripped from the corners of their finger-pointing mouths. By Eve's testimony and Adam's testimony, Eve was sweet jelly in the sin equation because she took from the serpent what she should not have taken and gave to her man what he should have declined. It doesn't always happen but notice what God did. Since Eve was by her own admission the sweet jelly between two pieces of bread—Adam and the Serpent—God tied both redemptive and punitive responses to both pieces of bread. Be sure to check it out in the text.

As the man, Adam was the God-appointed leader of the relationship, so there is no way to get around it because he sat down on manhood when he should have stood up as a man. And yes, the "fair play" insistent lens of the camera quickly pivots and focuses on us in the here and now because we enjoy beating Adam up, but we deny our sameness. So, yeah, I look back at that very first man, and yes, I want to claim that I'm much more evolved and further down the line of spiritual development, but I pause to ask, "Are men any more evolved?" Perhaps I can answer the question by asking a few questions:

For example:

1. Why have so many of us Christian men had babies outside of wedlock? Although we claimed Christ as "Lord," in defining moments when "brother orgasm" whispered wet promises, we failed to take spiritual responsibility for the wild immoral dog that wants to live within us. By not behaving as Christ in defining spiritual moments, we scandalized the name of Christ and left a residual "putrid mess" on the soft silky sheets of women's lives.

2. Why are Sunday school classes and weekday Bible studies dominated by women? When the time comes

to know our Bible tools and sharpen them, we routinely flip the blankets of responsibility off our shoulders and send our women out without us.

3. Why do so many of our daughters grow up and settle for "bad boys" or just plain losers who are neither good for them nor good to them? And further, as Christian men, how do we routinely rationalize that so many of our sons turn into men who can only be described as "wandering lost souls?" Dare we take active day by day and night by night responsibility for fathering our kids so that we produce kids who contribute as citizens of this world community and as impactful citizens of the heavenly kingdom?

4. If, by chance, we have women in our lives whose spiritual talk is greater than their spiritual walk, dare we take responsibility by taking them by the hand and leading them back to a more authentic "actionable" Christian life? Abraham had some good moments before God but, in a pivotal moment when Sarah was itching for God to produce a child they had been waiting on, Abraham failed to properly balance his

dealings with his wife with the need to obediently rely on God (Genesis 16). You see, some of us can get blinded by the delicate beauty of her hand when we should be focused on the stuff in the hand that she's trying to feed us. Let me try to say this more directly. If your woman is full of crap, recognize the crap and don't eat the crap. Determine to address the crap as directed by God.

5. Dare we as men take responsibility for the children of the world? Yes, I'm talking about our children's friends with absent fathers who we routinely walk past in the neighborhood, at our kids' sporting events, and at church. Can we ask ourselves whether we have just a little extra love, care, wisdom, and discipline that we can offer a child whose own absent "sperm donor" has misread his responsibilities?

In Gen 2:17, we witness God placing the mantle of responsibility directly in Adam's hands regarding which garden tree to not eat from. In my sanctified imagination, the succulent beauty of Eve must have almost outshined the sun as she stood before Adam with fruit juice sweetly dripping from the corners of her luscious lips and offered him the fruit. I don't mean to be unduly hard on Adam, but like you and me, he needed a better sense of the moments in life that scream for good, wise, and responsibility-based questions.

Week 16

GodIDon'tUnderstand

Genesis 4; Proverbs 17:17; Proverbs 18:24

1. God – I Don't Understand.
2. God, I Don't Understand.

Number 1 signals when a man has "a God he doesn't understand."

Number 2 signals when a man cries out to God "that as a man, he doesn't understand."

I have deliberately run the words together in the subject field. I can only imagine that both sentiments of each phrasing meshed together in the heart of Adam upon receiving news that his beloved son, Cain, had taken the life of his beloved son, Abel. Being a man and being a father, I'm guessing the gross circling darkness of grief oozed from his every pore. He was still new to the multi-angled canopy of human sin, and this was the first death he'd experienced. So, most assuredly, he must have been crushed and dumbfounded as despair carried him to the bloody scene where his son's lifeless earthly body lay in the dirt—battered, bruised, and eternally gone.

As I contemplate a few horrendous losses in my own life, I can't help but identify with Adam. As he contemplated the probability that while the new hurt would someday become an old hurt, he remained unsure and felt that he would never have the strength to face a new normal. I, and we, know what it's like to suffer debilitating loss and then have to turn to God and figure out whether we're going to praise Him despite the loss or scream curses at Him because of the loss. If it has not happened yet, be thou well assured that the possibility of your "God, I don't understand" moment can and will come. The text is eerily silent regarding how Adam managed to get up every day after that, but get up, he did. We know that because the record of his life indicates that Adam had more children, which means life, chores, marriage, and the like did, in fact, go on. How about you? As a man, how have you managed those moments? As a man, are you reasonably poised to handle incoming "God, I don't understand" experiences of life? Whoever you are, depletions, deletions, and reverses will always be on the menu of life, and unsure footing and spiritual immaturity will make it increasingly difficult to navigate those realities. Are you spiritually positioned for the loss of a home, the loss of a child to death, the death of a child-father relationship, the loss of a lover to death or the death of love even though you still live in the same house with her, the loss of gainful employment, the loss of respect for the institutional church, or the loss of the natural ability to perform sexually with your wife?

You have an advantage Adam didn't have. You are privileged to be a part of an international, intergenerational, and multicultural body of brothers. So, reach out even during your dizzying "God, I don't understand" moments because good brothers in Christ can help you to understand at least one valuable truth: Even when you're in a "God, I don't understand" place, God loves, knows, cares about, and understands you.

Week 17

It Can't Be Holy

Hebrews 13:4

Have you ever found yourself drowning sweetly in the ecstasy of pleasure and then suddenly felt the jerk of mental discomfort that whispered, "This can't be holy." The truth is this—the stamp of sin on our spiritual DNA often can cloud everything, and that includes the times when we should, in fact, rest and abide in the good things that God allows us! You see, the sin stamp often warps our instinctive interpretation of God and leads us to assume that He's one big killjoy of anything we take pleasure in. The most immediate example that perhaps comes to mind for a lot of men is the marriage bed. Even there, because of the stamp of sin on our spiritual DNA, we have some degree of difficulty viewing the buzzsaw of moist penetrative intimacy as a moment to spiritually celebrate God's wonderful gift. Although some men freely "call upon the name of Jesus" in those moments, He's actually far from our minds because we often wrongly and instinctively feel He has no part in such moments. In our unspoken hearts, we forget to lick the holy altar of God with a mind of worshipful thanksgiving. Instead, we sometimes instinctively feel it's appropriate to return to God after the act even though the truth is that God is the sanctioner and creator of the act and, might I add, present for the act. I'm grateful to the "real man" who wrote Hebrews 13:4 because it signals both a warning about violating the contract of the marriage bed by going outside of it and it also signals the rightness and righteousness of "Ah, Ah, Ah, Ahhhh time." In the context of marriage, it's not a dirty moment. It is a holy moment.

Your heavenly Father loves you as a man, understands you, and harbors no desire to deny you anything that's in your best short, medium, and long-term holy interests. So, as you look at life and as you look at the sometimes low hanging fruit of life, remember that the question is not, "What can I get away with," but rather the question is, "What's meant for me?" God has a goody bag like no one else and, if we nurture our relationship with Him, He'll point us to wow-wow experiences where the enjoyment of good gifts have no attached shame or dishonor. As men, let's learn to discover the goodness of God for us, grab the goodies of God for us as men, and freely ingest the pleasures that come with being the sons of God who fully love the wives that God has given us. Let's also not forget that God's good gifting of intimacy extends beyond the bedroom. Shared intimacy of hearts, the beauty of mutual goals, and the support of one another in life's endeavors further spur us to oneness in marriage.

With regard to the marriage bed, an old preacher still full of sexual fire once said to me, "What God has placed between the legs of a woman is so wondrous and powerful that it hovers among the three to five most phenomenal forces on the planet." Think about it. In the context of the sacredness of marriage, God has given you full possession. Let's push to override sin's influence which lies to us and tries to convince us that what God has for us isn't actually holy or ordained. It's both.

Week 18

Life Sucks?

John 14:1; John 10:10; Galatians 5:23

A desire for eternity is stamped into our DNA. So, since we want to be around forever and, in fact, will be around forever, we might as well displace our "temple of tears" perspective and push ourselves to the focus and value of God's magnificent glory. By the way, in case you don't realize it, we can say we'll be around forever because "after death comes the judgment," and after the judgment comes eternal life in His presence or eternal life twisting in the scorching fires of hell. Job said, "Man born of a woman is short-lived and full of sorrow" (Job 14:1). Although that's true, that's not mentally where we have to live. If negativity constantly camps out in your spirit, you need to know that God desires spiritual positivity to carry our wheels forward. That doesn't mean to live life in denial. It simply means that we latch on to the Rock of our Salvation because we know in whom we have believed and that He can keep us until the day of redemption.

Have there been moments when our reactionary instincts shamefully told us to cancel the breathing contract of a girlfriend, fiancée, or wife? Yes. Are there fleeting seconds when our kids make us wish we had worn a condom on the night of their conception? Yes. Unknown to them, are our employment supervisors dangerously close to seeing the sudden lethal appearance of the "Rambo" who lives within us? Yes. Do we occasionally desire to hide our aging parents' dentures because they think they can freely say to us whatever they're thinking without appropriate filters? Yes. Do we occasionally want to neuter the preacher because he constantly aggravates us by being mind-numbingly irrelevant? Yes. At least once in our lifetime, have we longed to offer a slow rhythmic locomotive "choo-choo" ride to somebody who shall remain nameless? Yes.

Yeah, a Windex-clean mirror of life or window to life can really suck at times because the compilation of who we are, what we want, and even where we've failed ourselves can be daunting. But let's remind ourselves that there is a reason that God has stamped a longing for eternity into our

DNA. He desires to be glorified eternally, and He desires for us to eternally have the exuberant joy of leaving behind the popping kernels of struggle that come with trying to be a righteous man while maneuvering the filthy tunnels of life. But wait a minute, because I would be wrong if I didn't mention John 10:10, "He has come to give you life, and life more abundantly" (in the here and now). When our perspectives are right, we understand that while some lemon juice gets squirted in our direction in life, we can still suck on the abundant wonderful fruits of the Spirit and then look forward to our eternal joy fest party in the eternal by and by.

Week 19

Moment of Impact

2 Samuel 12; Exodus 3:1–5; Matthew 5–7

I'm prepared to argue that God has sewn our "moment of impact" into the fiber of our souls. One might assume I'm referring to the moment that grace sweetly caught you by the throat and spun you into an heir of the King. That certainly could have been your "moment of impact," but for many other men, it does not represent their actual "moment of impact" by way of seismic behavioral change. For many years, King David raided more Victoria Secret panties than you could shake a stick at, but when David encountered God on the road of despair over losing his infant child, it was indeed a "moment of impact." He was never quite the same old David from that point onward. Although Moses understood his cultural heritage and the all-important special God relationship his ancestors enjoyed, it wasn't until God made him take off his blue suede shoes and stand barefoot in His presence that he had his true "moment of impact."

I was saved as an adolescent, and for many years, was steeped in the church. I was a professional at talking in church and even masterful at the superficiality of public "churchy" behavior. Yet, my raw fall on my knees, stop "playing church" impact moment didn't come until later. How about you? Have you had your true moment of behavioral impact yet, or are you still hanging out on the comfortable sofa of Christianity and ignoring the sights, sounds, and bloody stains on the cross? Some "men in church" are so clueless that they don't even immediately recognize the difference between operationalizing Jesus as Lord versus just claiming Jesus as Savior. So, let me offer seven hints to help us assess whether behavioral impact has occurred:

1. If neither private nor group Bible study ever seems to routinely make it onto your busy schedule, and you still claim you've had your impact moment, you're full of "poo-poo" and should soft-pedal that claim. For you see, a truly hungry man will claw his way toward some

food "come hell or high water." Contrary to what you claim, the actual problem is not your schedule but rather your poor appetite for the Word. The impact is pending.

2. If prayer is pretty much only something you do on Sunday morning when everybody else bows their head or when a crisis arises, the impact is pending.

3. If kingdom service is optional for you, or you do it only to check the box, please your wife, fool your girlfriend into thinking you're actually serious about spiritual things, or to keep the preacher from looking at you disapprovingly, the impact is pending.

4. If nitty-gritty Jesus-living is only attempted in the company of nitty-gritty Jesus-people, the impact is pending.

5. If you still hold the conviction that your money is your money, the impact is pending.

6. If your kids still see and smell the stench of hypocrisy wafting from the peepholes of your life, values, and attitude, the impact is pending.

7.   If you're frequently and intentionally dismembering and assaulting the basic dignity of others who dare to disagree with you, that is quite probably a sign that impact is pending.

Men, if we're going to be in this thing, we might as well throw down the hammer and chase the devil out of our thinking, out of our homes, out of our work, out of our churches, out of our playtime, out of our wallets, out of our movie collections, out of our dating experiences, out of our struggling marriages, and out of the non-biblical ways we raise our kids! For sure, Jesus calls ordinary men to live extraordinary lives, and that's not a dreamy prospect only known in a heavenly scenario. Back here at the ranch where we daily live, we should be operating like hungry men! Hungry for what? We should hunger for a moment of true impact!

Week 20

Legs on Fish

1 Corinthians 5; Romans 1:18–32

The summons to monogamy was hardwired into the human imprint, but the vortex of sin threatens to swallow any thread of belief that suggests we're not destined to bump and grind every willing victim that moves in a skirt. Without the unction of the Holy Ghost, sin's translation of masculinity becomes both ingrained and irrational. The despicable situation in 1 Corinthians 5 is a good example. The man was sleeping with his stepmother, and the irrational rationalizing of sin was so bad in the church that folk were either looking the other way or outright condoning it. Paul was so upset when he was informed of this man and woman's audacious and diabolical actions that he responded with declarative fire! Yep, a man and his stepmom slipping and sliding between satin sheets, as if it were completely legit, gave Paul a severe case of spiritual heartburn because there are norms of spiritual righteousness that can never and should never be viewed as negotiable.

You see, Paul felt it was important to honor sacred things, and these two folks were announcing to sacred things, by their behavior, that all sacred things could kiss their "horny butts." The indecency of their sex nest was an offense to God, an offense to their local body of Christ, an offense to the broader public witness of Christ, an offense to the man's dad, an offense to their individual commitments to God, an offense to their collective families, and an offense to church leadership.

Among other things, herein lies a major part of the problem. It's convenient for everybody if we all throw up our hands and succumb to the secularization of the church, which in part means holiness should not be preached and, if it is preached, don't actually expect it to be lived. Certainly, if we collectively treat holiness like it isn't what it is, we can more easily both believe and behave as we choose. It's akin to the ridiculous proposition that if we say it long enough and loud enough, we can get everybody to accept the notion that "fish walk around on legs." Romans

1:18–32 suggests that mankind constantly attempts to suppress and repress the reality of God, which has been stamped into humanity's DNA. When a Christian man attitudinally does his wife wrong, at some level, he understands instinctively that he has also done his God wrong. When a Christian man manipulates his way into or accepts an offer to fall into the luscious, pulsating "happy place" of a woman he is not married to, the postmortem spiritually smells like a rotting dead body even when the behavior isn't widely known. Likewise, when a man cheats his employer in some way, he also understands that if nobody else ever knows, his God knows. When a man repeatedly comes up short in attending to kingdom business, despite the seemingly airtight wall of reasonable-sounding rationalizations, he knows that His God ain't buying it.

While Paul was hard on this man and the woman in the text, once again, I must admit that I, too, have needed to crawl from beneath the weight of the audaciousness of sin that was occasionally done boldly in the light. As I visit with the long arc of sin-bends and review that man's need for a spiritual prison break, I'm compelled to confess what both he and I have denied even while knowing we were in denial. The rough and tumble sea of sin has a way of repeatedly dunking a man in the well of alcohol even after a man admits to himself the habit has taken more from him than it has given him. We don't dare justify the sin of the man in the text, but we understand this man because we, too, know how sin can wrap itself around the neck of a man and momentarily feel soothing before the pain sets in. We understand that man because we know instances when shame built a tunnel around us and fleetingly shielded us from the embarrassment of moral turpitude. We know that man's denial because we've had friends who, in the end, didn't behave friendly toward our souls. Although they knew better, just as we did, they didn't speak the truth to our situations. Yeah, the man in the text stubbornly pushed ahead with his behavioral filth, but in the end, he still knew that fish don't walk around on legs, and we know that, too.

Week 21

Be the Girl

Psalm 139; Romans 8:28; Isaiah 40

God has built "finiteness" into our DNA. Yes, God has built us to be chest-thumping warriors, large and in charge, but, as men, we must wisely reconcile ourselves to what we still can and cannot know about God because we are finite. You see, sometimes I am pleased to know that I am fully known by God, but I'm also willing to admit my occasional frustration that God is clearly outside of the reach of being fully known by me. Even though we're finite and don't always know what we don't know, we should occasionally strive to review the intimate detailed knowledge God has of us. For example:

1. He's so into us that He even monitors the details of the what, when, where, and how of our dream lives. Yes, while we're lying comfortably in the darkness of our beds and our subconscious minds take flight—for good, ill, or neutrality—God is there. In fact, in the Scripture, God occasionally

invaded the slumbering stillness of a man and met with them while they dreamed. I am thinking of Joseph, Jacob, Abraham, Samuel, Solomon, and Daniel. For sure, sleep is what we see as perhaps our most vulnerable state. God occasionally uses it to speak unto us deep truths, dig up in us some needed transparency, and even help us see what we haven't been able to see while our eyes are wide open.

2. When we do the right things for the wrong reasons or do wrong things with the right intentions, God is there and knows the real deal. Both Abraham and Moses knew something about that. For Abraham, among other soft spots of his humanity, God knew his heartache was to have a son. For Moses, God recognized that all of the majesty that came with being a part of the Egyptian court could not hide within Moses his own fragile awareness that he couldn't speak with eloquence.

3. While we may be enamored by the wonderful willingness of "wild Wanda" to wet our whistles at any time, any place, and in any position, God understands that "sweet Sarah," who is a bit timid

compared to "wild Wanda," is actually what we need. God understands that for many of us, at some point, we'll wisely arrive at a place of realization that wild Wanda was only built for good times, but sweet Sarah can stand strong through the bad times.

There was a time when I saw the phrase "eleventy one," and it left me scratching my head because there was no surrounding context, and I still don't know what it meant. However, it occurred to me that the person who placed it there knows exactly what it means. Often, God will leave us wondering about "eleventy one" in our lives, and He feels no obligation to explain what He knows. Yes, there are things—small, medium, and large—that we cannot know, so we must practice the discipline of embracing our finiteness. Here are two fundamental things that you can know:

1.   God loves you.
2.   God can and will if you let Him take care of you through all of the complexities and challenges of life. I want to be like the little girl I saw in a Walmart store recently. Yes, you heard me. I want

to be like that girl. Her father had several heavy bundles he was carrying, and among those bundles, there she was nestled close to his chest and sound asleep. You see, instinctively, she knew she could trust Him to do his job, which at that moment was to understand her positioning and reliance and to carry and keep her safe despite whatever else he was dealing with. Let God be the Father, and you be the girl.

Week 22

Free at Last

John 8:32

"She doesn't care about truth as long as I do what she says." Those were the words of a little girl as she described the unhealthy texture of her relationship with her mom. God has stamped a desire for earnest truth within our hearts but, when the blinding soot of a life that is uncomfortable with truth builds up, it requires proactive spiritual work to get to a place of preferring truth over a lie. The Scripture speaks a lot about truth and the importance of truth. While teaching in the Temple one day, Jesus went on a truth rant that even the religious leaders of the day found to be scandalous. Jesus tied truth directly to knowledge of Him and being in a relationship with Him. It must have been a barn-burning moment when Jesus said, "Know the truth, and it will set you free" (John 8:32). If you don't actually know the truth, it means you're like a mangy, caged dog that foolishly chases his tail in circles. There are lies about God, lies regarding the divine trajectory of life, lies about identity, lies about what masculinity should be like at its core if it's to accommodate shifting cultural norms, lies about one's worth, and perhaps even lies that displace the centrality and function of the church.

Interestingly, even incessant liars get aggravated when they find out they've been hoodwinked, bamboozled, taken for a ride, and told a lie. Yes, there is something in the "higher ideals" of the human spirit that prefers truth over a lie. So, when a man spends much of his lifetime peddling small, moderate, or big untruths, he eventually finds himself in the basement of life staring in a mirror at a man he barely knows the truth about.

It's hard to explain, but we instinctively understand that truth often ushers clarity to the doorstep of our lives. It empowers us to comfortably look beyond what we cannot know. Truth provides a level playing field that allows us to make informed decisions. Truth lifts up the skirt of life and shows us what we honestly need to see even when the sight of it pinches our tender mental and emotional nerve endings. Once again, however, I must mention the "dark passenger" known as sin because sin barks growling demands at us and insists we turn our God-assigned man spiritual attire inside out and pretend we're looking normal. Have you ever left church feeling squeaky clean and airbrushed even though you're still actively waddling around in a personal bucket of sinful slop? That squeaky airbrushed feeling suggests you've managed to compartmentalize in a way that keeps objective truth at a distance from incessant untruths, and that's a dangerous place to be. Have you ever left church with spiritually aching bones, screaming toes, a spinning head, and your heart pounding with a compulsion to repent, surrender, and be better? Do you understand that if you allow God to more fully engage you, doing better follows closely behind? That feeling suggests you're in a better place than the first squeaky airbrushed dude because when your heart reacts to the truth of the gospel, it means you're better positioned to be susceptible to the truth of the gospel! It means you're in the neighborhood of freedom. It means the truth about you is about to have more appeal to you than a lie about you, a lie to you, or a lie from you. When you arrive there, pull out your microphone and prepare to thunder from the steps of the Washington Mall, "Free at last, free at last, thank God Almighty, I'm free at last!"[iv]

Week 23

Man Secrets

Psalm 51

Most of us can identify a woman in our lives now or in the past who seemed to have an eerie ability to stay two steps ahead of us. Yes, somehow, some way, she managed to peer deep into the inner sanctum of our hearts and minds and clearly see the dirty walls that lined the unspoken intention of our wills. While we didn't openly say what we were aiming for, and though we initially disciplined ourselves to fake gentleman-like behavior, somehow she knew we were hell-bent on someday licking her morality down to the bare bone and mercilessly circling back for seconds. Somehow and some way, she knew the smile on our face and the charming, sweet rhythm of our words were secretly laced with the powerful venom of a cobra bite in search of satisfaction. Somehow, she knew fidelity and true lasting respect of her honor and best interests sat a million miles away from the humping, thumping, and delicate caress of our generous compliments. Somehow, she knew behind the fancy clothes stood a skeletal frame of a guy who was, in reality, a take-only and self-absorbed straw man. If by chance, we struck sexual gold and got to lie on the soft cushion of her bosom while sniffing the intoxicating sweat from her body, we nervously wondered how long it would take before our flesh turned to glass and she was able to see anew not just into us but straight through us. While we resented what her mother warned her about us, it was only because we felt like empty vessels who are impaled, impaired, and therefore ill-prepared for a substantive and meaningful love relationship.

Somehow, that woman knew that when we answered yes in a strong, assured masculine voice, the honest truth was still no. Somehow, she knew we were only at church out of obligation to her, tradition, our public moral reputation, or because it kept our parents quiet or the preacher thinking well of us. Behind the sheen of our male armor, we've secretly asked ourselves, "Who am I? How long can I keep my deep hidden father resentments a secret? How much longer can I keep up this good boy image when the truth is I'm joyfully rotten to the core?

How long can I maintain this image of fearlessness when the raw truth is that life scares me? Why can't I seem to say what I mean to the people I love? Why can't I seem to mean what I say? Will my penis always be my leader even though I intellectually know I should be his leader? What am I to do when my wife and kids leave me drowning in the sea of their neediness almost every day?"

Of course, the above does not detail every man's journey, but it does strike with familiar reverberations for many men. Here are the words of King David at a key moment in his life when his latest secret fell from the revealing sky and opened a cavernous hole around his feet for all to see:

"Be gracious to me, O God, according to Your lovingkindness; According to the greatness of Thy compassion blot out my transgressions. Wash me thoroughly from my iniquity and cleanse me from my sin. For I know my transgressions, and my sin is ever before me. Against Thee, Thee only I have sinned, and done what is evil in Thy sight, so that

Thou art justified when Thou dost speak, and blameless when Thou dost judge." (Psalm 51:1–4).

I could talk all day about that real man, David, who struggled for a good portion of his younger years to be a true friend to God but, yes, he did get there. There is so much to contemplate in the above words from David's mouth, but I'll resist a highly detailed dive and simply point this out. That, in my view, is the most transparent prayer in all of the Old Testament. It is evidently a secretive man who has chosen to acknowledge his life has not been an open book, and at that moment, He invites the light of God to shine in the icky crevices of his carnality. It is a secretive man who now understands that he desperately needs the graciousness of God even though he had a reputation for being a man of greatness. David was a man who understood that although God was first in line by way of being offended by his sin, others were impacted by his sin.

The context was different, but the paraphrased warning of Moses to Reuben and Gad's sons stands as a clarion call to be men of honor, men who keep their good word, and men who don't hide in the dark what will surely come to light. Moses told them, "Your sins will find you out." (Numbers 32:23).

Week 24

Reading His Own News

Psalm 1:1

A few years ago, I read an article about a killer who dismembered his victim and then meticulously began to eat the body parts as if enjoying a bologna and cheese sandwich. Being unable to resist the potential of fanfare and attention, he then posted his sick acts on YouTube. The article suggested that he reveled in the worldwide electronic attention and that he spent countless hours "reading his own news." That phrase, "reading his own news," immediately caught my attention.

Hopefully, none of us have the sickening proclivity of the criminal I've referenced, but most assuredly, we know what it is to be drawn to the "reading of our own news." Reading our news typically involves one of two extremes: 1) either we've pressed our ears, eyes, and hearts to the loudspeaker of life and listened in to the blaring or subtle diatribes of what never has been and never will be; or 2) we've repeatedly listened to the chorus of praise and applause for what people "think" we are regardless of how far it may be from whole, authentic truth.

As I glance back at the long road of my Christian journey, I can find moments of acclamation wherein I was looking shiny and fine. Contrary to what I wanted God, enemies, the church, and friends to think, I was actually struggling not just with doing right but, more importantly, I was struggling with even "wanting" to do right. Psalm 1 says, "Blessed is the man who does not walk in the counsel of the wicked; blessed is the man who does not stand in the path of sinners; blessed is the man who does not sit in the seat of scoffers." Bing, Bam, Boom! For sure, my struggle was even more shrill than the screams of my critics, who occasionally managed to catch glimpses of my inner dark personal passenger. For you see, I wasn't just failing. I was failing at trying to not fail. In fact, I think the psalmist should have added my name at the beginning of verse one because I can point to a time when at least three things were true in my life:

1. I took a certain measured delight in walking in the well-oiled slick machinery of unwise counsel. Most especially when it pointed to the hidden backyard of the pleasure principle.

2. I enjoyed the sinner's path because it was often littered with tasty morsels along the road, contrary to what I heard some preachers preach.

3. I quietly applauded my "bootylicious" seat with the scoffers because it "seemed" apparent that I and we had repeatedly stared down the threat of divine justice and had survived to do it yet again.

The hot and steamy private Twitter blogs might tell true stories about the unchecked violence when you slapped the taste out of your woman's mouth for defying you. They might tell stories of occasions when you beat another brother down simply because making him look small helped you feel big. They might tell stories about your prowess at illegal gambling and how you lined your pockets with money, money, money. They might tell stories about your legendary reputation during your military days and the wild things that happened when you were granted leave from the base. They might herald your college days and the wild stuff you pulled off with your fellow Omega dogs. But, alas, reading your own news headlines minus the power and presence of Christ will always eventually leave you unsatisfied with the abiding reality of you. Instead, read His news for you in John 10:10.

Week 25

Scooby–Doo

Exodus 3:2; Timothy 1:7

A great line is nestled in an old Theodore Roosevelt speech called " Man in the Arena." The excerpt says:

> "It is not the critic who counts, for the credit belongs to the man who is actually in the arena, whose face is marred by dust and sweat and blood, who strives valiantly. His place shall never be with those cold and timid souls who knew neither victory nor defeat."[v]

I did a quick word study of the simple word, "fear," and was reminded that fear is typically defined in two ways. Fear can be innate, but it can also be identity-based. Innate fears are largely universal to humans. That is to say, that type of fear comes from a virtually universal desire to avoid certain things like pain, death, or falling from a high mountain. Identity fear is different because it's linked to desires to avoid things like embarrassment or rejection from others. Fear, in my view, often fuels timidity.

Moses from the Old Testament is often heralded as a man's man, a great leader, and a great lawgiver. However, a closer look at his life reveals a man who, at defining moments, stood on the precipice of self-doubt, inactivity, and timidity. Yes, there were moments when this extremely gifted man flirted with the possibility of life's impotence, and he, like us, had moments when he was virtually consumed by his own self-doubt. Yes, like us, he could also be missing in action for, in multiple defining moments along the way, he swung to a place of almost insufferable fear and paralysis.

In Exodus 3, God personally introduced Himself to Moses with great power, fanfare, and historical self-explanation. In response, the first words out of Moses's mouth were sadly filled with self-focus and self-doubt. Even as the conversation expanded and God filled in additional details of what would be, Moses responded with the typical spaghetti-weak male response when we want to avoid the possibility of trying anything great. That response was, "Well, what if?" Yes, we frequently use the "what if" response to sidestep trying anything that involves the smell of greatness.

I don't mean to offend his fans, but Scooby-Doo was a bad Christian role model for other dogs because he was too often a timid wimp who always had to be coaxed into flashes of courage (smile)! One day I noticed that one of my ministry partners, Rev. Robyn McCoy, has a quote at the base of her email communications that says, "You are not defeated until your doubts take the place of your dreams." Just like Moses and just like the timid Scooby-Doo souls that Roosevelt referenced, the truth is this: we men of God at times can be mushy, soft flowery peddles of nothingness even though we have power access to be spiritual Ninja Warriors capable of beating demonic forces that come up against the name of God, the sanctity of the family, the purpose of the church, and the cause of Christ in our individual walks. Yes, we often secretly wrestle with a timidity that paralyzes our God-given mandates to storm the city gates and encircle communities with righteousness. Our timidity creates in us a woeful passivity when our sons need us to speak about righteousness in their lives.

The Scooby-Doo type of timidity triggers an unwilling-
ness to pray with our wives for fear our words won't come
out right. Timidity causes us to sit idle when Uncle Joe sits
at our dinner table and tells off-color and inappropriate
jokes. Yeah, when the God of ministry desires to use us,
we always have a reason or an excuse for why we can't
speak up, step up, straighten up, reach up, and produce.
The Apostle Paul saw timidity as a pitiful Scooby-Doo
behavioral pattern. He reminded us, "God has not given
us a spirit of timidity but of power, love, and a sound
mind" – 2 Timothy 1:7.

Week 26

Expedite the Crash

Exodus 3; Exodus 12

It's hard to explain the timing of God, but it does at least appear from the human angle that there are times when God will expedite a crash. Yes, even though it may appear from the human angle that the moving object of nonsense and disbelief is nowhere near a stationary blocking object, God can nevertheless step in and interrupt the mess, seemingly out of nowhere. Yes, God can interrupt the mess of stubborn unbelief or self-belief, which is actually still unbelief when out of balance. God can interrupt the mess of single people's sexual escapades. God can interrupt the deep unholy groans of a liaison between adulterers even before they try to shower away the scent of sin. God can interrupt the Christian believer's sad, quiet quest to steal from Him by giving way less financial support for kingdom work than he or she ought to be giving. God can interrupt an angry petition to file for divorce. Yes, God can interrupt all the messes that can come in life from different angles and expedite crashes. Think about it:

- Moses escaped the warrant Pharaoh had issued for his arrest because God interrupted it.

- God interrupted Moses out in the remote Midian wilderness where he was having hot sandy sex with his new wife and making babies. That was not because Moses was wrong but because God wanted him to change his location to lead the birth of a new nation.

- Although Moses was acting as the chief operating officer over his father-in-law's business, God interrupted Jethro's business because Jethro also had a new calling to utilize his people management insight and be an advisor for God's business.

And then it happened. God expedited a crash! Crashes can be first-time introductions to the stunning realization that God does exist. Still, crashes are often also transformative moments for believers when He engineers dizzying circumstances, shocking events, confrontations, paralysis, dreams, desperation, and heartbreak to further expedite His designed purposes in their lives. My surrogate little brother, Rev. Dr. Christopher M. Jones, contends (and many would agree) that "Covid -19 has been a God expedited crash for the globe," which of course also means the institutional church has experienced a crash! Luckily for Moses, instead of setting Moses on fire, God instead chose to miraculously set a bush on fire which was still a crash for Moses. And life for Moses suddenly took a hard but fulfilling right turn! I choose to refer to that as an expedited crash because it seems to me that Moses was already fully engaged in a good life and might have been tempted to argue for a delay in how God expedited the crash in his life.

David knew something about crashes. After all, he was just a boy when the prophet Samuel showed up and signaled an impending crash. Speaking of Samuel, he knew something about crashes because God expedited a crash in his life by situating him as a temple resident even though he was just a young boy. Samuel's situation prompts me to underscore that crashes often occur with small audiences, not large audiences. Samuel's parents and the priest Eli were the only ones included in the inner circle of Samuel's crash, and initially, the adults didn't know the full extent of the impending crash.

Keep in mind that whether your natural abilities are viewed by you and/or others as ordinary or extraordinary, whether you or others view your past and/or present as qualifying or disqualifying, God can grab any man and expedite a crash regardless of whether you're shiny or downright dingy. Although Moses had his goofy moments, I love that he allowed God to completely alter his life's pathway. After all, he could have lived the comfy life in an Egyptian high-rise luxury condo but, alas, because God expedited a crash in his life, he traded a high-rise condo fit for an Egyptian prince for dusty overcrowded tents in the wilderness.

Men, sometimes God expedites a crash into our lives, and life looks nothing like it once did. Sometimes God expedites a crash into our lives, and it abruptly changes how we define friendship. Sometimes the crash will alter how we manage our time, and it leaves little room for things that were once important. If you lean in close and look at the crash that God expedited in the life of Moses, you'll see the rudiments of incredible life enlargement for Moses. Don't miss that because crashes that are executed by God will result in an exciting spiritual adventure that involves high stakes! The individual pathway God has set for each of us places each of us at the intersection of good and evil, life and death, and spiritual greatness and human diminishment. Even though we initially might be a little unsteady like Moses, let's send a signal of willingness to our sovereign God that we're willing to submit to the crash.

Week 27

Man On Fire

Psalm 121:1–2

One day I listened with interest as a man described how he felt whenever he went to see his girlfriend, who lived at a great distance. He explained that the closer he got to his sweet stuff, the more he felt on fire and about to melt. The thought of a man on fire caught my attention because the reality and effectual impact of "fire" and even the symbolic thrust of hostile fire-like situations and circumstances cannot and should not be ignored in our lives. One of the great honors of my ministry years has been to connect with men along the winding road where masculinity can be both beautiful and littered with tough battles. Although nuanced because every man is an individual, the experiences of men do have some common threads. Here are a few common fire-filled thematic sweeps I've encountered from masculine voices over many years. I've included a few instances when the concept of "fire" is used positively. However, I've often seen positive fires go south, so I've attached representations of those experiences as well.

- Vocational weariness: Anger management has admittedly been a struggle all of my life, and last month I came close to "busting a cap" in the supervisor's butt because right is right and wrong is wrong. The Lord Jesus came close to needing to bail a brother out of lockup. I was on fire with rage. I was so enraged I was about to burst into flames on the spot where I stood. As I see it, my work is me, so when my supervisor degrades my work, he degrades me.
- Sexual frustration: Before I got married, "nasty Nadine" seemed to instinctively know how to pleasingly pop a brother's eyeballs with her undeniable sweet-sweaty rub of sexual shock and awe. Now, Juanita (the wife) gives me resentful looks even if she thinks I'm thinking about some sexual playtime with her. The simple truth is I'm tired of the dry toast visitations to my bedroom, and I'm about to burst into flames because of it.

- Sexual disinterest: I've been there and done that with my wife many, many times, so I now have no interest in it nor the energy to do it. The flame is gone. Wish she'd leave me alone.

- Unknowable things: I love exploring the deeper truths of the Word of God that can be known and understood via Holy Spirit enlightenment and rigorous study. Such truths have only aided my spiritual worldview, and they helped me see culturalism through a biblical lens and showed me the intricate hand of God in human history. In time, I've also admittedly grown restless about the increasing number of big questions that the Bible doesn't answer. In the domain of God-given intellect, it's inexplicable to me why a God who portrays Himself as highly relational and communicative chooses to and without explanation remains silent in critical areas of needed revelation.

- Unrealized dreams: I am not who I thought I would be at this juncture of life, and in the midnight hour, my emotional head quietly hangs in debilitating sadness and self-disapproval. I love my kids and my wife, but the honest, raw truth is that the reality of them has diminished the reality of me, and I'm about to burst into flames.

- Evangelistic fervor: My zeal and hunger to see others come into a relationship with Jesus were explosive and widespread. Certainly, the pastor could count on me for anything at any time because I understood the critical nature of the mission, and to say I was on fire for Christ would be an understatement. That was many years ago, and I must now admit that the rainstorms of life and the shocking failures of those who were my leaders have left me disillusioned by the inadequacies of the institutional church.

Whether you're a Christian brother wrestling through the dating stage and trying to properly manage the intoxicating call of your girlfriend's womanhood, or you are a man seething with anger about life's regrets. The Word of God puts forth a straightforward remedy for all of the potential explosive triggers of life: Look to the hills from whence cometh your help - Psalm 121:1–2.

I love that strong, straightforward nugget because it signals a recognition that fire exists and where help can be found. There are times when we should stubbornly shut the front and back doors where our rationalizations enter and just do what the Word says before we burst into flames or do what the word says as a means to extinguish existing flames.

Week 28

That BIG Butt

Romans 8:1; 12:1–2

So, it was previously mentioned that some Christian men bear the secret of not wanting to even try to do right. Yes, that's right. With one hand, they routinely give God their middle finger. With the other hand, they finger the delicious, although temporary, sweet, satisfying taste of sin even while burping and emitting its poisonous odor, which they think nobody notices.

Other men, however, actually want to do right but get frozen by the painful memory of man overboard funky failures. With the clap of mental and emotional thunder, the devil parachutes down into our lives and tosses a bomb that we then allow to pry loose our grip on growing spirituality. Then he grabs us in his teeth and violently shakes us like Mike Tyson would do to any man who dared slip him a kiss on the lips. For many of us, that has not just happened once but multiple times over the years.

We've tried to spiritually rise only to have sin's messenger dope slap us back to the ground like we were nothing more than scared underage girls in the raging grip of a muscle-bound wrestler.

Our response to sin's messenger, the devil, is akin to a cowboy who's been thrown off his horse so many times that he stops riding. He simply stands around behind the horse, sheepishly staring at the horse's butt instead of mounting it and bringing it under control. You see, the unpleasant sound and feel of his backside thumping the dirt or pavement have sadly convinced him to not try again. That's what the devil is hoping for in your life. He's hoping previous attempts and failures at having a truly substantive relationship with Jesus the Christ will leave you standing around staring at the proverbial icky crack of the horse's butt.

My dear brother, I admonish you to divert your gaze from the moist, leaking crack of the horse's butt and push three truths into the forefront of your spiritual memory bank:

1. There is no condemnation for those who are in Christ Jesus. Yes, that's right, if you've genuinely met the Savior and accepted His offer of Salvation, you are safe and sealed for eternity. Romans 8:1. I know you recently undressed the associate pastor's drop-dead gorgeous wife with your eyes and allowed yourself a brief, delicious moment imagining what it would be like "to do" her. Yes, I know you've been carrying deep-seated hate in your heart for a family member who did something to you years ago, and you still haven't recovered from it. So, mess-ups and screw-ups, while not pretty, cannot/will not/shall not cancel your "hallelujah I made it" appointment at the foot of heaven's throne.

2. We fight not against flesh and blood but against spiritual wickedness and principalities (Ephesians 6). That is important because you will continually fail to see the real issue without that perspective, which results in a misplaced battle focus. Yes, let's be careful because it's easy to misidentify the enemy, which often results in a carnal perspective

and reaction to a spiritual problem. Let's remind ourselves that spiritual forces are behind relentless poisonous gases that spill into our marriages. Remember, spiritual forces behind the creeping secularization of sacred acts tell us it's perfectly normal to offer our approval to our son's marriage to Robert.

3. The absence of being transformed necessarily signals a certain comfort level with being conformed (Romans 12:2). Make no mistake about it; the longer you plant your feet and flirt with the leaky, oozing, smelly crack of life's butt, the easier it becomes to passively accept, dangerously ignore, or even begin to like the sight.

Men of God: Step away from the butt!

Week 29

What's Your Name?

1 Kings 19:1–2; Job 2

Sometimes truth can be completely unsettling and, so, here's a secret truth: I don't consistently know my name and, chances are, you don't either.

You see, God created something incredibly dynamic and explosive that exists between a man and a woman. On the one hand, her mere existence exudes a pulsating, intoxicating, lovely, soft, wise, caring, and nurturing attraction to all things. Yet, on the other hand, her existence can also exude a calculating, emotional, unreasonable, stubborn, and manipulative intimacy power grab of all things. On either end of her possible feminine wiles—and in-between—our secret is that we tend to lose sight of our best God-defined masculine selves. You see, whether she is right or wrong, we are supposed to remain in touch with our God-given identities as men. We move, submit, yield, pull, push, stand up, speak up, and shut up only at God's command rather than at the command of a Victoria's Secrets promise of a head-bobbing, toe-curling, tongue-speaking orgasm. Sometimes we're simply spineless because we don't want to risk the temporary loss of her electric sexual plumbing. Still, sometimes we also simply don't want to experience the cold silent freezer burn of a sister with an attitude.

Like us, our women are both saints and sinners, but as men, we often fail to spiritually note the moment and the identity, which means we fail to properly act or react to the feminine identity in any given moment. As a man, I must ask myself, "Who am I," or, "Who am I most like? Am I Ahab, or am I Job?" King Ahab was an ungodly leader of God's chosen people and was married to Jezebel, who operated with a scorched earth policy. Yes, Jezebel would cut your throat and sip your blood through a rainbow-colored straw while cheerfully singing Aretha's song, "Respect." Yes, she was the First Lady of God's appointed nation, but nothing was holy about her. After Elijah's great victory over Ahab and his theologically confused prophets, it's very telling that the text immediately says, "Now Ahab (even though he was the

King) told Jezebel all that Elijah had done." Then Jezebel sent Elijah a message that said (paraphrased), *"Sucker, I'm going to do you in."* (1 Kings 19:1–2).

On the other hand, Job lost all that he had, including his material things, and even worse, his children. Yet, when his wife suggested that it was insane to still praise and honor God, Job pushed back with righteous indignation and sucked his teeth so hard that he almost lifted the gold-plated fillings from his molars. "Woman, have you lost your cotton-pickin' mind?" I'm struck by Job at that moment because he cared enough about the righteousness of God to reject his wife's unrighteous viewpoint, but I suspect he also cared enough about her to confront her because she was dead wrong. Don't miss that. Care enough to confront. So, in the face of feminine power, I must ask each of us as men, "What's your name?"

Week 30

When God Ain't Godly

Psalm 73

Here's another secret that throbs inside the chest of a man. I'm almost scared to say it out loud, but here it is: There are instances when I or we feel God is simply not godly enough. The Psalmist, Asaph, stood flat-footed initially and told the truth about what he saw going on right under God's seemingly questionable godly nose.

Yes, that's right, there are times when God miserably fails to line up with our human expectations of Him, and that includes our need for Him to cooperate with our desire to see Him execute devastation when we think it ought to be so. Yes, at times, the simple truth is that God's godly version of His godliness fails to satisfy our sometimes carnal expectation of what He ought to be. The sometimes disillusioned questioning of our hearts sounds something like this:

- We ask, how can we, as men, TRUST a God who allows injustice after injustice to crackle, crunch, creep, and crap around our feet without rapidly straightening things out with a clap of thunder from His supposedly mighty hands? After all, how credible is divine might when it is kept in pretty wrapping paper while all hell is seemingly breaking loose in every tribe and nation?

- We ask ourselves, "How can we as men trust a God who would allow the death of someone close to us even after we've emotionally petitioned Him publicly at open mic night at church?"

- As men, we ask ourselves, "How can we depend on a God, who isn't godly enough to grant us the dream job we had hoped for and others were sure we'd get?"

- We ask ourselves, "How can we place faith in a God who idly sits by and lets another man lure our wives from our beds to his bed and not then cause them both to have some really nasty affliction that causes certain body parts to rot and fall off?"

- How in the world can we trust a God who doesn't seem to know what time it is and, therefore, repeatedly fails to show up, show His power, and protect His own credibility after being mocked by unbelievers?

- We ask ourselves, "Why does God allow some churches to linger in the land of financial struggle when other churches that are far less faithful to the mission of Christ are bustling and bursting with fiscal fat, activity, notoriety, and gobs of people?"

Yeah, Christian men often secretly feel that God ain't so godly. But here's the thing that the biblically fragile folk and the spiritually concrete legalistic folk will find it hard to hear.

God is not like Mr. Clean, who insists on being tidy and sterile with clean straight lines for all of life. Rather, the truth is that God, the things of God, the moves of God, the allowances of God, the decrees of God, and the timing of God can actually look messy and can be messy when viewed through the limited lenses of our human perspectives. In the end, His righteousness, power, and glory flow like mighty streams of water, but again, often time, the superintendence of God does not have the look of a straight, simple line.

When the dirty funk of life and the complexity of our God overwhelms you, read your Bible like a starving man looking for the nourishment of truth. Psalm 73 is a good place to start.

Week 31

Squirrel Butt

Ephesians 5:11

In too many instances, the secret is that we don't know that the secret isn't much of a secret. What am I talking about? I'm talking about the alleged secret that I personally carried many years ago, which was that I stunk. Yep, I spiritually stunk like a squirrel's butt on a hot and humid Mississippi day. Yep, went to church every Sunday. Yep, I even served as a young leader in the church, but I still spiritually smelled like hot garbage from hell's sanitation bin. How about you? Do you stink? Nope, didn't ask about your church title nor even how much you financially give. Let me ask a few tough, direct questions that may quickly reveal whether you dwell in a spiritual deodorant-free zone.

1. Do you have a sanctified mind, or is your mind often saturated by stuff that would shame your mama, enrage your spouse, embarrass your kids, cause your spiritually mature friends who love you

to hold their noses, and deeply offend your holy God?

2. Would your local church where you have membership be in good shape or terrible shape if every member operated with the same level of commitment as you? Additional questions in this specific area go something like: Is God's mandate and the preacher's vision really the problem, or is the real problem that the church has too many members who are like you? Are you full of hot air with reasons why you regularly starve the ministry of your service and gifting? If your pattern of financial giving was the gold standard, would the ministry immediately collapse because of a lack of support?

3. Is your wife constantly suffering under the weight of you being a spiritual lightweight? Are you and perhaps your mate constantly working to sharpen your rationales for what ain't right about you both but ought to be?

4. Are you a secret-agent Christian? That results in a Christian home that's reasonably moral but not actually Christian. It results in an employment

situation where co-workers are quite surprised when they stumble upon the discovery that you go to church. It results in scenarios where neighbors want to know where you go to church because they'll be sure to avoid that church. Its consequences include a household of kids who know of Jesus, but they're not even remotely close to actually knowing Jesus.

For sure, we cannot earn grace by looking to our own righteousness to get us brownie points with God, but that does not mean we should casually and nonchalantly stand before the Father and just outright stink like a squirrel's butt. God calls for a church without spot ("stank") or wrinkle. Paul said, "Do not participate in the unfruitful deeds of darkness." Ephesians 5:11. In other words, Paul doesn't want us to be known in the spiritual realm by the initials, "S.B."

Week 32

Brother Delicious

2 Corinthians 5:17; Romans 8; 1 Corinthians 15

The demonic hosts whisper in hushed tones to one another as they slither into the shadowy cavern where their weekly briefings occur. Mission: "Our father, the devil, needs us to sweetly suggest to human men what they ought to do because he's hoping to keep them from knowing what they can do." You see, men, demonic hosts know that it's hard to control a spiritual man-lion when the man-lion discovers his God-given strength and submits to routine training on how to employ his God-given strength.

Yes, as God's lion-like man, what are the nitty-gritty practical implications of the truth of who you are and what you're capable of?

Implication #1: You become a targeted man. Indeed, the devil's job is to minimize your manhood or use your manhood, assuming he can't successfully influence your death. If the devil can get you to actively live a life of milky compromise, he successfully minimizes you. If he can get you to "fake-care" about spiritually healthy things or be a sandpaper irritant to spiritually healthy things, he successfully minimizes and uses you.

Implication #2: The world notices you, fears you, but doesn't fully understand you even though it may claim otherwise. Yes, like Paul and his cohorts, the reality of your manly presence serves as an uncomfortable notice that an unusual somebody is on the scene and employing unusual convictions anchored by a belief in a power that is anything but usual. Don't get it confused because often, that will also mean you are also despised by those who carry devilish agendas in their bosom.

Implication #3: You have the power to say no to the allure of Brother Delicious (Satan). Yes, you know Brother Delicious very well. He occasionally attacks your dream world around 2:00 a.m. with wild blasts of vivid regurgitations of sugary moments that should never have been or he influences dreamed imaginings that should never be. He tries to momentarily blind your otherwise clear sight of the fact that you should wait on God and not rush ahead with what you want based purely on logic. He tries to get you to exchange transformative biblical truth for a self-serving delightful lie. The whispers of Brother Delicious tell you that things are hopeless because the black hole you're in has no bottom.

Despite the tactical lies and slick bent truths of Brother Delicious, here's the absolute truth. The implications of who you are in Christ means that, despite previously being as guilty as a whore in church without panties, you can still approach God with confidence because when in Christ, the blood of Jesus covers and secures.

Yeah, sometimes our secret is that we don't actually understand the implications of being sons of the risen King!

Week 33

"Your Reach Should Exceed Your Grasp"

Psalm 51

One of our secrets is that we are often not deep thinkers. We allow the strong, forceful current of life to toss us and take us along with its natural ebbs and downward flows, and we often fail to grab the tree branches of life, pause, and catch our breath. There's no doubt about it. Life can be a busy complex intimidating beast but here's the thing. A Christian man who fails to be a deep thinker will regularly get caught in the squeeze and underbrush of life's natural elements, sweeping him out to the sea of superficiality if his mind is not sharp and infused with godly wisdom. Put another way, our modern world and the devil's incessant slick attacks are too fearsome for us men to allow ourselves to be intellectually lazy, dumb as bricks, big-belly horny fat cats.

Since my teens, I've long been fascinated with King David of the Scriptures. He was a true renaissance man.

He was a musician, a warrior, a leader, an organizer, a Shemar Moore-type ladies man, a poet, and more. Among his most important qualities was the fact that he was also a thinker. He was not a brother who spent his time sitting around watching the mindless ying-yangs on the hottest talk show. Although he was very human and had at least one jaw-dropping fall to your knees weakness, he was still a brother who routinely and seriously contemplated the longitude and latitude of life, living, and lordship. In fact, in his well-known fifty-first Psalm—which was a repentant tearjerker after he got busted for playing hide the sausage with another man's wife—he said to God, "Behold, I was brought forth in iniquity and in sin, my mother conceived me. Behold, Thou dost desire truth in the innermost being and in the hidden part Thou wilt make me know wisdom." Yes, although those are the words of an imperfect man, they are still the words of a man who was a deep thinker.

Robert Browning said, "Ah, but a man's reach should exceed his grasp, or what's a heaven for." That simply means one should reach for more than they can easily see or get their hands on. However, in far too many instances, we flip it and only reach for what we can see and tangibly touch. Men of God, press and reach for a richer life in your intellect because God has given you the capacity to imagine and grasp a lot of great things that sometimes only appear to be beyond your grasp. Deeply engage your woman in conversations that are more than the question, "What's for dinner?" Or, "Are you going to delight me tonight with the "wanga-wanga-woogie-woogie?" Require your children to become thinkers about sacred and social issues, philosophical pondering, and even political thought. Also, don't lazily settle for sitting under preaching that fails to inform, challenge, inspire, and convince. For, if the preacher never causes you to scratch your head over lofty thought or you don't want to hit him over the head because he's challenging your mess, simply put, he or she ain't worth a bag of spit. Lastly, learn the importance of taking time for quiet thought and talk with the God of the universe. Yes, let your reach exceed your grasp and you'll discover that you're able to grasp even more.

Week 34

Boy in progress

Psalm 51

Boy: Hops and skips along without a thought of a godly identity.

Boy in progress of being God's man: Occasionally thinks about it, and occasionally or frequently dips his toe in the water but has not jumped in.

God's man: Stands naked with feet firmly planted with outstretched hands and says, "Here am I Lord. Use me."

We men have a reputation for love-hate relationships with medical doctors. When I moved from Massachusetts to Virginia, I noticed my new doctor's progression in his dialogue and dealings with me. The conversation started at a surface level but it got really personal in time and so did his examination! In fact, at one point, I had to wonder whether that man desired to date me! Seriously though, guys, I've been drawn back once again to my main man, King David, because he was so brutally raw in his communication and self-disclosure with God that it almost makes me want to blush like a little girl.

You know, my doctor almost always did at least two things that I didn't appreciate. First, he almost always got personal and, second, he almost always said things I didn't care to hear. The Spirit of God moves upon David's heart in Psalm 51 and leads David to fling open his kingly robes, spill his guts, recognize some things, reconcile himself with some things, and otherwise give God glory for all things. Before that, however, and given the mountain of female panties that David implicitly devoured, it's hard to believe not one of those women attached to the panties ever shamed David by signaling their disappointment for his early failures to answer the divine summons to be a man of God.

What I like about this "too honest for church" prayer is that it frames where David is, which in turn signals where he had been. Make no mistake about it. At that juncture in his life, it was a heart-emptying exercise for

God's man. That was not a boy or a boy who was only in progress toward being a man of God. That–was–a–man– of–God!

This is how you can tell:

- Only God's man invites God to execute a get real, get clean, wash the dirty dimples off my butt, naked cleansing (verse 2).

- Only God's man who has, in fact, sinned against others as well recognizes that ultimately, his greatest putrid sinful offenses have actually been against God Himself (verses 3–4).

- Only God's man seeks a radical heart transplant wherein his old heart gets replaced with a new one (verse 10).

- Only God's man has a desire to submit to a total makeover so that he can then take it and teach former co-transgressors what they can look like, smell like, and be like (verses 12–13).

Are you a boy, a boy in progress, or are you God's man?

Week 35

A Temporary God

Philippians 2; Hebrews 9:27; Revelation 20

Whether it's at work, home, church, life's playground, or the shadowy inner lining of our manly-thought lives, we often act like Stanley Cup goalies. We're expected and we expect ourselves to keep pucks from landing, dwelling, and gumming up the nets of life. Yes, we've become quite adept at quickly kicking out solutions to problems. In addition to other corners of our manly souls, that pattern often leads us down the path of what is nothing more than an illusion. Yes, our secret is that we actually get lulled into sometimes thinking that we're large and in charge of what can be, will be, and must be. However, when a substantial mind and gut check happens in the life of a man who has actually met God, he finds himself standing on the shore of the following inescapable and somewhat perplexing human truth. Either we can live in the reality of the all-powerful eternality of God, or we can live in the reality of the all-powerful eternality of God. Yeah, that's right, it's a double vision situation because whenever a man finds himself standing alone and spiritually butt-naked in the presence of God Almighty, the man eventually comes to understand that the sovereignty of God creates a one-way thoroughfare for creation. So, whether a Christian man lives for God and eventually steps into the domain of eternal life in the glorious hallelujah presence of the living God, or whether a non-Christian man eventually steps into the domain of eternal life in the scorching, scarring tunnels of hell, every man eventually dwells in the reality of the all-powerful eternality of God.

God is not temporary but, rather, eternal, which means none of us can sidestep and avoid the divinely scheduled appointment. Yep, even if you've given God your heart, mind, soul, and body, you still have a face-to-face—stand naked and stand at attention—appointment with God to keep. If you've refused to acknowledge His existence, you still have an unavoidable appointment. If you once served Him but backed off to do life your way, you, too, have an inescapable appointment. If you're an impostor who only goes thru the religious motions of knowing and serving God, you, too, must keep your appointment. If you're the kind of man who believes there is likely some type of energy or force in the world that is larger than mankind but is not identifiable, you've got an appointment. If you're the kind of Christian man who has decided you're going to raid, rub, slap, tap, wax, pull, and poke as many panties as you possibly can while you can, or freely swim in the ocean of some other unholy perversion and worry about the consequences later, all I can say is this one word, "appointment." If you're a functionally moral man but frankly rarely gives such lofty thoughts even a passing thought, you too have an appointment.

How can I, a mere man myself, declare with such absolute unwavering authority what shall happen at some point on the mysterious eternal runway of God's long view? The answer is simple. I can say it because the Word of God unapologetically declares, "It is appointed for every man to die, and after that, comes the judgment." Hebrews 9:27.

If you're in Christ and I don't get to meet you on the often slippery boardwalk of this life, in the eternal by and by, I'll may see you somewhere near the judgment throne of the eternal God because after all, "It is appointed . . ."

Week 36

Lick It, Stick It, Hold It

John 15

Love can change what you want. I keep being taken back to the provocative words of Jesus Himself when He said, "By their fruits, you will know them." Matt 7:16. You see, it's not what my friends say about me that best defines me or what my enemies say but, rather, what best defines me as a man is first what God says about me and, secondly, what I honestly and objectively say about myself. Let me help you connect the dots by adding this thought. It's not my words about me that best define me but, rather, it's the desires of my heart that say something quite truthful about who I am at my base core and where I'm headed in the development of my spiritual humanity over and above the sticky-icky rub of my human carnality.

If you are a man who has put considerable mileage on the car of life which includes what you've done, thoughts you've wholeheartedly ingested, and emotional and situational wreckage you've endured, then you can now look back—assuming you have some spiritual maturity—and vividly see that love can change what you want. Yes, some of us can now look back at the tricky, itchy crabgrass of polluted relationships that previously meant so much to us and should not have. We can hardly believe those previously toxic connections were voluntarily held close to our chests. Yes, some of us can now look back at "jump on it juicy Judy," who delivered untold repeated moments of hair-raising sexual explosions and now we clearly see that she actually affected and infected us with a long-term mental abscess in the darkened corners of our manhood. Yeah, some of us used to rest on what we saw as the trustworthy and unfailing rock of scientific reasoning but we can now look back with a decisive understanding that science doesn't hold the answers to all things but, rather, God in Christ holds the world in His hand.

So, what's the key to obtaining a GPS system that will lead you away from the stain of your prior self and the other unholy allurements of life? The answer is that you must learn to fall in love with Jesus. That means spending time with Jesus in the Word and building a practice of honest talk with Him, listening for signatures of His voice, intentional time learning from more mature believers, and reviewing His purposes for the world and your purpose. Giving yourself in kingdom service and discovering your gift are all avenues that will escort you to a growing place of love. While our bend toward sin is obviously a problem, the more specific problem is that we don't love Jesus more than sin. Authentic, substantive love of Christ will bring you home to a place of spiritual grounding and will begin to cause you to be repulsed at the thought of a raw, naked offense against Him. When you get to a place of mature love, you'll discover that much of what you used to want and even felt you needed begins to diminish in varying degrees in its push and pull on your heart and mind. Indeed, true love for the Master can change what you want.

Week 37

Dead Men's Shoes

John 15

Oftentimes, we are steel-toe leathery erect creatures who would rather burn than bow. Our mothers, wives, girlfriends, sisters, and daughters can often serve as witnesses for how stubborn, resistant, and bearish we can be when someone or something smacks against the deep throat voice of our manly and sometimes carnal wills. How many times have we vocally or behaviorally said to something, somebody, some principle, or some issue, "Kissa ma buttocks". In the self-prison that I'm capable of creating, I ask, "Will I always live with the admission that I am not who I once thought I was and must I also live with regrets that I will never be who I'd hope to be?"

Men, all too often, we secretly sneak our old mentality into the domain of our relationship with the Lord Jesus, hoping that no one will notice. Lately, I've been doing some honest thinking about what the Lord is calling me to and I've been really honest with myself about how my fleshly side wants to respond to His command. Here's the uncomfortable truth about where we often find ourselves when we face the funky spiritual path of what I'll call "Must Boulevard." We often choose to treat Christ and the commands of Christ like we'd treat a dead man's shoes. We'll look at them, acknowledge their presence, perhaps assign a degree of admiration to them because of who previously wore them, and even perhaps stick them in a special place. However, let's be clear because for many of us, they will not be put on our feet and worn. We must face the following daunting truth. Jesus calls us to upset strongholds and overturn the sour, wobbly tables of this increasingly new world order but we simply cannot fulfill His calling unless we're willing to walk in the shoes of the Lord who died for our sins but who now lives.

In the fifteenth chapter of John, Jesus laid some heavy stuff on His disciples as He prepared them for His death. Yeah, John 15 provides a quick look at some crazy Jesus shoes we're required to wear if we are at all interested in sidestepping the spiritual pain of a constant state of spiritual impotency. Jesus says, boys, if you want to be real men, listen up:

Verse 2: Spread your spiritual legs, grunt and give birth. That's right, you can't claim to be a kingdom producer if you're not a man who routinely gives birth and bears fruit. When your wife and kids are away for the weekend, your character demonstrates the presence or absence of you bearing fruit. The consequential impact of managing your money for kingdom purposes is a very real demonstration that you are or are not bearing fruit. When you find yourself compelled to share the gospel with another man who doesn't know Christ, that's indicative of a man who is bearing fruit. When you use the good, bad, and ugly of your testimony to help another believer, that's indicative of fruit. Yes, the uncomfortable pruning process is a necessary measure to help us bear even more fruit.

Verse 10: Slap, hot air boy. That's right, one of the true measures of a man comes down to whether he is a "muscle-bound hot air boy" or whether he is a "choke the pee-pee out of the devil and just-do-it kind of man." So, if you're little more than a church-attending guy who is filled with useless hot air, you need to spiritually slap yourself and step toward the thunderous impact of spiritual masculinity. Real men of God don't just talk a good talk. They walk the good walk. In a culture that pushes the primacy of individualism, it's a battle to acknowledge the Word of God when it signals there are "must do" and "you will do" truths that are sewn into the thread of an authentic Christ relationship. Certainly, our loving Christ's expectations point to non-negotiables and to make negotiable what Christ signals as a non-negotiable is a non-starter.

Verse 12: Love, Bubba. This question must be asked and answered. Are you able to love your fellow man no matter his cultural context or are you only able to politely smile and tolerate other men who aren't naturally or culturally your cup of tea? The broad tent of Christendom has all kinds of culturally diverse men and for sure, we have to reach beyond cultural likes and dislikes if we're going to successfully connect with other men both in and outside of the body of Christ. In fact, learning to love someone who falls outside the cultural enclave you know, love and are most comfortable with may very well be the bridge that better shows you the beauty and power of the international move of God among all tongues, tribes, and nations. When we men make the mistake of painting God as a "stars and stripes American," we tragically miss the bigness of God that transcends political ideation, cultural relativism, ethnicity, and, yes, even capitalism.

Verse 18: Hug the hate. Yep, if you want to actually walk in the Master's shoes, you've got to be ready to earn and accept the hate for where walking in the Master's shoes will often land you. You accept the hate by reminding yourself that the world's hate for Him necessarily means hate for you. Now, if you're clearly in a place where there are never any haters buzzing the pathway upon which you walk, it's time to look around a bit closer because you are clearly not walking heavily upon the street that aligns with your God-given identity. Perhaps we should occasionally thank our haters because they in part assure us we're on the right pathway.

Verse 27: Holla. Yes, to walk in those holy big shoes, you're required to courageously tell the story of Him and the story of your love for Him. Often, people might be inclined to be quickly dismissive of your theological musings but it's less easy to be dismissive of your story. Men, tell your story that entails what it has been like to be with Jesus, to learn Jesus, to love Jesus, to trust and obey Jesus, and to be a witness for Jesus.

The beautiful thing about each new day is that you can start it and end it with the shoes of Christ.

Week 38

Chick Flicks

1 Peter 1:13–25; 2:1–10

For many of us men, the problem with chick flicks is that they're often slow and always filled with syrupy, tear-filled, eyeball to eyeball uncomfortable emotional confrontations and entanglements. While on vacation with my sugar britches, this truth came back to me yet again as we sat through another chick flick. There were no bone-crushing punches thrown, no pints of blood lost, no cool severed tongues, no intestinal spillage, and nor were there any cool instruments of death. Contrary to those who don't know what they don't know, if you read your Bible, you'll quickly discover action that indeed captures the hearts and minds of battlefield warriors all the way to the imaginations of titans of industry and all men in-between. The Word is so timeless that it even includes ancient forerunners to Jason Bourne, Rocky, and Superfly.

As I watched that great chick flick about a marriage that lost its way, the marriage's underlying principal problem quickly became clear. The problem was not that a cosmic, transformative event occurred in the marriage but, rather, the problem was that unannounced rot had progressively fueled poor behavioral patterns. As men, a few of us have experienced a sudden traumatic event in our spiritual lives somewhere along the way and it successfully strong-armed and pushed us off the path we had previously used as a means to chase after God. Still, for many of us, it has not been sudden claps of negative events that have derailed us but, rather, slow, quiet, and progressive rot just like I saw in the chick flick marriage.

Here are some possible secret examples that we prefer to not talk about:

One: We suffered the gradual loss of inspiration because a spiritual leader left us or let us down. Or we let ourselves down because of a series of life-altering dumb decisions and, consequently, we left our true selves. Yes, before we knew it, the shadowy push of dusk had turned into utter darkness, and eventually, we had to admit we were still walking, talking, and barking but we were dangerously lost.

Two: Some of us up grew up in the pit of nothingness with parents and other adults who deposited very little quality into our lives. So, the truth is that we've been in a natural downward slide toward the base of the worst of our untamed humanity for all of our lives. Although Christ saved us, the long-entrenched pattern of embracing the ugly and worst side of ourselves keeps raising its ugly head. Yes, it's really hard for us to truly believe that the words "goodness and mercy" can be for us.

Three: For some men, the usual vestiges of unrighteousness are not and never have been their primary problem because they were raised in the church and, for the most part, they've always done what their straight-laced mommy and daddy told them. They've carried themselves in a respectful churchy way and never even been directly exposed, for example, to really good porn. Yes, they are the poster boys for the goody-two-shoes award. If anything, their problem is actually self-righteousness, not unrighteousness. Although, if the truth be told, self-righteousness is actually a form of unrighteousness.

In all three examples, it's important to understand that rot is typically slow, quiet, and progressive. From the lifting wind tunnel of God's Word, my counsel is simple: Latch on to some God-ordained action and attack rot perceptively, aggressively, methodically, honestly, and prayerfully. Knowing Jesus means you have Holy Ghost-inspired tactics to employ an attack against the danger of spiritual rot. Here are a few well-worn ways to enact the attack. There is nothing especially insightful about them but, when operationalized, they have proven to be effective time and time again in the lives of believers.

1. Get yourself under some regular good preaching and teaching and eat the Book! That is an old drum I've been beating for many years because good spiritual eating is critical to good spiritual health. Let me slip in a potentially controversial insert. The devil is real and life comes at us in real and tangible ways, so to sit week after week and listen to pastoral preaching that is soppy, milky, and a guaranteed sleeping pill is tragic. Additionally, remind yourself

that good biblical teaching is not just about information. It's also about an escalation of your elevation to greater spiritual revelation. Take responsibility for the quality of the spiritual food you're being routinely served and when its nutritional value is lacking, seek better.

2. Search for a solid relationship with someone stronger than you to walk the path of life with you and hold you accountable. I've mentioned that a couple of times throughout the book because it's fundamental to our spiritual growth but it often doesn't happen. If you don't have someone pouring into you, especially if you're on the spiritually younger side of the ledger, storm the throne room of heaven with your petition and watch and wait. By the way, don't lie to yourself by telling yourself you have no such need simply because you've been around church since the beginning of time. Why? Because there are plenty of men who've been around church and Christianity for many, many years but are still spiritual babies. At least in part, because they've never had a spiritually mature man to teach them

and walk with them along the road of becoming a spiritually mature man.

3. Work at developing a meaningful prayer life. The goal here is not to sound like the preacher in the pulpit when he or she prays, but rather, the goal here is to simply open a bidirectional line of frequent communication with the Father. A prayerful man is a man who has God's attention. A prayerful man is a man who is willing to tell God the truth. A prayerful man is a man who will gain insight into the moves of God. A prayerful man is a man who can switch jobs with confidence because he doesn't move without the approval of God. A prayerful man grows to rejoice in God's "no" because he understands that God's "no" is just as much for his good as God's "yes." A prayerful man is a man who doesn't say yes to whatever a church asks of him simply because the church asks but, rather, he says yes only when he believes God says yes. A prayerful man learns to thank God for the woman God gave him rather than fixate on the woman he could have gotten for himself. A prayerful man understands that his spiritual gift and

potency in ministry are given by God and can be withdrawn by God. Before talking to wifey, mother, father, sister, brother, or pastor, a man of prayer understands he needs to first talk to God. A man of prayer understands that prayer also involves listening for God's voice, over against one-directional talking to God.

4. Get off your rationalizing excuse-filled butt and get onto the field of ministry action. There is nothing wrong with golf and other activities that many men enjoy. However, when anything displaces a God assignment, it becomes a wrong involvement. The aim of our lives is to glorify God and that should take priority over our recreational interests. Notice I didn't say our recreational interests have no place. As men, we have to carefully calibrate our lives to honor our God, honor our wives and families, be vocationally responsible, nurture friendships, and, of course, also give appropriate attention to recreation and re-creation. When men carefully balance their lives, the summons to ministry need not file a missing person report and thereby leave women forced to pick up the ministry slack.

5. Don't forsake the benefit and joy of regular fellowship with the people of God. Although still imperfect, substantive people of God can be and will be wonderful and enriching additions to your life and the lives of your family members. Please notice that I said people of God and didn't say church attenders or church members. While they might be ok, they won't and can't bring to the doorstep of your life what muscular people of God will bring. Connect. Trust. Contribute. Share. Nurture. Partner. Seek. These words and more are signals of what it means to be a part of the worldwide body of Christ.

You know, chick flicks aren't that bad. On top of the drama, there are usually rivers of suggestion about the importance of healthier relationships. Fraternities, sororities, athletic clubs, business networks, and the like all have their value. But do not try to live an isolated Christian life absent the life-altering fellowship with other believers.

Week 39

Bitter Fork

John 14:16–18

When you're eating your spaghetti and your teeth come in contact with the fork, you don't try to power through but, instead, you wisely release and avert your grip. For any man who does attempt to power through, I have a simple question, "How's that working out for you?" You see, God has given us the Holy Spirit who works to guide and sensitize us to that which makes sense in the spiritual realm and that which does not. Yes, to have a fundamental understanding of truth and to live a life that's largely aided by spiritual wisdom and insight is a great comfort to the heart of a real man. I suspect you're not too different from me and that you likewise find yourself occasionally caught and squeezed by both the subtle and not so subtle grips of modernity. Do I ignore the Word and grab on to new truth that suggests I should, in fact, switch my pronoun usage to call Bill "her" instead of "him" because he's decided to now identify as a female?

Should I betray biblical standards and instead grip newer expressions of marriage that involve not two people but three? Without truth in your heart, you'll continue to mimic a wild, insane dog who repeatedly tries to power his way through a steel-plated bone (the fork) even though delicious eatable food is also right there for the taking.

As men, our secret is that when our spiritual tanks are low, we actually do try to power through stuff even as the Holy Spirit flashes neon blinking signs in an attempt to get us to avert our stubborn grips. Time and time again, over the years, the Holy Spirit spoke and told us not to be blinded by how deliciously hot Betty's booty was and, therefore, miss seeing how dark and horrendous Betty's heart was. Alas, we stubbornly attempted to power through even though Holy Ghost signals warned of moral degradation if we insisted on grabbing it, playing with it, and exuding pride that we had it. In the end, we loved it until the sweet-stanky stuff noticeably and spiritually infected us, left us, or eventually lost our attention. Time and time again, the Holy Spirit took us by the hand and began to lead us down the path of safety and immunity from the buzzsaw of self-imposed foolery. Alas, in too many instances, we stubbornly pulled away, admired ourselves in the mirror of life, and insisted on pretending we were the embodiment of self-determination. In some instances, we dumbly distanced ourselves from the very people that God would have used to grow us, challenge us, and hold us accountable. We refused to release our grips on a mentality we should have sidestepped. Time and time again, the Holy Spirit beckoned us to a standard of biblical holiness that would have left our wives drunk with the pleasure of being connected to a man whom God Himself bragged on. Still, we politely ignored the beckoning and stood on the street corner of moral blandness and vanilla churchianity that fails to be consequential.

Yes, some men grew up in church but the church's best teachings didn't adequately grow up in them. They now find themselves standing across the street from their church experience, quietly throwing rocks at the God of their salvation. It's at least in part because they've grown accustomed to relying on their own understanding and mistakenly thinking they have the power to hold their grip on the carnal pretenses of manhood. Even though the

Holy Spirit calls on them to release and avert their incredibly dumb grips. Failing to avert an unwise and ungodly grip will result in a marriage being less than it could be, with children being raised to be less than they should be, with ministry involvement that tastes like warmed-over plastic. It will assure an unfulfilling walk with Jesus that feels like He's walking on the west coast with you walking on the east coast. Stop! I repeat, stop biting the fork and instead taste His goodness, experience His power, depend on His guidance, enjoy His protection, and relish the sight of His glory.

Week 40

God's Daughter

Ephesians 5:22-33; 1 Corinthians 7;
Matthew 5:27-32; 1 Peter 3:1-7; Song of Solomon

I did not marry an angel, but I did marry God's daughter. I've been thinking and chewing anew on the above well-known Scriptures on marriage. The truth of the matter is that the pondering of marriage is never far from my heart and thoughts because I'm fascinated by human behavior and I've been joyfully privileged to live in marriage with one of God's premier daughters for over thirty-three years. My personal tendency is to end self-celebrations early and start asking myself and others burning and intrusive questions. For you see, as a man, I've arrived at a place spiritually where I judge myself to be reasonably decent as a man and husband. BUT, given who God has paired me with, plus knowing what God Himself expects of me, I'm compelled to ask the sometimes frustrating question, how do I get better? As men, we constantly battle the sometimes loud, and at other times quiet, twisted murmurings of this world order. As a man of God, my challenge is to not swallow what post-modernism teaches. Instead, I must continually bathe myself in rudimentary thought and questions anchored by biblical values and thought. For example: when I approach sexual intimacy as a Christian husband, am I propelled by Hugh Hefner's Playboy cosmetic imagery and soundtrack, or do I see sexual intimacy as an opportunity for a husband and wife to bask in the glory of God's good gift? Put another way, who do I really want in my bed? Do I want God's loving daughter (who does, in fact, handle her business), or do I want lopsided vain and profane Lola who fails to connect sex to the God who created and authorized sex?

As men, we're easily found guilty for often putting our heads down, mindlessly coloring within the lines of habit, while hoping our comfort zones don't get changed. But again, we need to remind ourselves that women tend to be more dynamic and fluid in their evolvement. Consider these additional thorny questions that men could consider asking and go in search of answers. When my man-like tendency tires of the female propensity for verbiage, do I slip into an ungodly 1950's Archie Bunker mindset or do I lovingly push pause to thoughtfully absorb what God's daughter wishes to share? Am I actually the spiritual LEADER in my house, or am I a weak figurehead who is contented to be a taillight pretending to be a headlight? While I'm happy to touch my wife physically, I ask myself, am I ever positioned to touch and positively move her emotionally? Do I ever cause her to have to reach up to catch up with my spiritual height, emotional depth, high-minded generosity, and kingdom service? Do I know the WORD of God better than she does, or am I still satisfied to rely on what she knows to be a guide for our life, love and leisure? For single men, must your "lady friend" singularly carry the weight of trying to bring some faint form of holiness to the relationship, or are you as a man standing up, stepping up and speaking up for "What thus saith the Lord?" And how about our tongues? As men, we must ask ourselves if we've learned to guard and guide our speech when talking to God's daughter, even when we're good and pissed off at her. We must even ask ourselves if we're being intentional enough in our celebration of her intrinsic value, career achievements, personal growth, and distinct approach to looking out for others. Are we giving deliberate attention and care for the issues and people she has a particular affinity for? Yeah, I'm PUSHING myself to bathe in the Word and be led by the Spirit. It would be great for (my) God's daughter to be able to say more than just "I'm married to a fairly nice guy," but rather, I want her to be able to say, "I'm married to God's son who causes me to be an even better, daughter of God."

Week 41

I Went Looking Again

Judges 13–16

After talking with a man recently, the question came to me, "Haynes, what are you looking for?" As men, we tend to not understand the difference between suppression and displacement. Yes, men typically suppress growing rot when what we really should do is work to displace it. I mean rot such as anger, resentments, unresolved conflict, deadly memories that won't die easily, and even festering sexual fixations with what we can't have or shouldn't have. Samson is a fascinating example of the mix of manly goodness and male insanity. When I review his life and times, it occurs to me that he was actually a microcosm of his time and people, the Israelites. That is to say, just as the people of God had repeatedly demonstrated ridiculous patterns of chasing unauthorized pleasures and setting them aside, only to later re-engage, here, too, was a man who made the mistake of not understanding the distinction between suppression and displacement. It's a nasty quagmire, but the simple truth is that we are often little reflections of our times and/or our family dysfunctions. That includes the unsettling truth that we can even be little unhealthy reflections of the "dysfunctional-ism" of specific local church communities where we've grown up.

Just before the announcement of Samson's birth, like dark poison ink in a well of words, Judges 13:1 empties itself onto the page of the holy writ with these exhausting words, "Now the sons of Israel again did evil in the sight of the Lord . . ." I would contend that this opening line aptly describes the path the greatly flawed servant of God would also take. Yes, although Samson had great possibilities and would become legendary, it is also true that time and time again, he would be found momentarily suppressing his appetites when he should have been working to displace them. As you review the record of his time, take notice of his positive possibilities but don't ignore the seeming insanity of situations that ring familiar for good reason. He kept returning to dangerous fires to play with again and again. Additionally, be sure to mentally note the twenty-year span of his rule as the judge over Israel and think about the ramifications of a man who incessantly digs virtually the same behavioral hole over many years, even as the consequences desperately yell to him to stop digging! Yeah, the results were tragic.

Yes, although our humanity never leaves us, we actually do have the possibility of growth and spiritual depth that will leave us far more sheltered and protected from vulnerabilities that previously would have left us flat on our backs! I suppose others would put the emphasis somewhere else and possibly articulate the angles differently, but this is how I choose to sum up Samson. He made the manly mistake of suppressing rather than displacing and that, in turn, repeatedly hurled him toward the wild field of hungry self-interests. You see, when you suppress, the filth that is inclined to attach itself to your character doesn't depart. It simply lies dormant for a while. When you work to displace filth, the gritty, nasty sweet peas of life are thrown overboard and made to feel unwanted. Don't miss this as well: men and women can't effectively displace the nasty sweet peas of life without filling the heart and head with the love, forgiveness, holiness, and power of the Triune God! Yes, intimacy with God translates into less comfortable space for the nasty sweet peas of life. Although sin can sometimes look as if it's an external agent that comes to find you, the greater reality is that we often go looking for it because it hangs out in the deep recesses of our hearts. James 1:13–16. So, solve the suppression-displacement distinction and you'll be well on your way to "not (routinely) looking, again."

Week 42

Too Fat to Fight

Matthew 16; Revelation 1

For some of us, the challenge of weight gain is a problem. In some instances, weight gain is not a problem and it may be needed depending on your physiology. I've read that there is such a thing as good fat. In the spiritual realm, however, I'm concerned about what I'll call bad fat. By my definition, one example of bad fat is when our knowledge is plentiful and our experience substantial, but our actual insight about Jesus is quite limited and misapplied. In the earlier section of our text, in rapid succession, Jesus posed two show-stopping, cosmos-tilting questions to His disciples: 1. "Who do men say I am?" and 2. "Who do you say I am?". An aggregate response was given to the first question. Peter singularly jumped out front and thundered his response to the second question. Oh, what a ground-shaking response it was!

"Thou art the Christ, the Son of the living God." It's not textually clear whether the next conversation with the disciples happened immediately or a little later. However, it can still be said that the next conversation reveals what I'll term as a display of how bad fat can have the right motivations but be wrong in its understanding. So, yes, Peter jumped out front yet again, but his informed perspective was dead wrong! The consequential result was that Peter got rebuked by Jesus big time and, yep, in front of everybody. Ouch! For those of us who've been around and have acquired substantial knowledge and experience in the things of God—like Peter—therein lies a clear warning. There can be times when our fat—knowledge and experience—can lead us to be certain about the will, and the will not, for how the Triune God moves when it would be better for us to slow our roll and be more open to ingest truths that may be hard to digest. For sure, in the text, Peter must have wished he had not told Jesus what could not happen. Peter was one of the three principal leaders among the disciples but take notice of how Jesus used Peter's fat-infused knowledge-stumble to offer a corrective muscular teaching response. So, we fat guys should lean in and take notice of what Jesus had to say.

1. **Come after me**. Yes, Jesus says, "If anyone would come after me.." I would suggest in these words, Jesus highlights the need for CONTEMPLA- TION. Yes, the pivotal lead word "if" points to the need to think, consider, and contemplate what's involved when a man says Jesus, I'll come after you.

2. **Let him deny himself**. In these words, Jesus is speaking to the need for RENUNCIATION. Indeed, disowning and divesting self of prioritizing people, places, and things that outshine the centrality of Christ will be necessary to effectively participate in the Master's agenda.

3. **Take up his cross**. In these words, Jesus was call- ing Peter and the boys to a place of DEDICA- TION. Bear in mind the unpleasant overarching subject of the conversation regarding impending suffering and death. Yes, it was necessary for Jesus to again underscore the importance of dedication by raising the specter of individual crosses.

4. **And follow Me**. In the pronunciation of these words, Jesus leaned toward ending the conversation

with a refreshed and throat-grabbing INVITA-TION. For sure, those of us who are fat with experience and knowledge should keep stepping through spiritual doors that capture new and deeper insights. We should fight the dangers that can subtly escort us to a place of unimaginative, stale Christian professionalism that eventually darkens our sight. For sure, we need to keep the skills of active duty warriors and resist resting on the laurels of yesteryear's victories and knowledge acquisition. Impressively, although fat with experience and knowledge, the elderly Apostle John on the island of Patmos allowed Christ to yet again blow his old mind with new understandings of the eternality of a new heaven and a new earth (Rev 21:1).

Even as a very senior agent in propagating the gospel, John was not too fat to fight. Are you TOO FAT to fight?

Week 43

A Casual Vacancy

Ephesians 1:15–16; 1 Corinthians 7

The truth, the whole truth, and nothing but the truth. Although we often don't like it, that is what the Word of God insists on giving us. When John was imprisoned on the island known as Patmos, which was off the coast of Asia, and he was caught up in the Spirit and recounted hearing a loud voice telling him to write, and write he did. Seven churches that were spread throughout Asia Minor were the targets of divine sweet missiles that came straight from the One who sits upon the Throne. The general thought pattern was as follows:

    1. Commendation

    2. Complaint

    3. Correction.

I've always been quite taken with the succinct words directed to the Christ-followers in Ephesus. (Haynes translation) "*I know your deeds, that you toil and persevere and that you can't stomach evil ding-dongs. I also know you call supposed apostles on the carpet and make them put up or shut up. You've hung in for My name's sake and have not grown weary.*" Wow, what a strong commendation. But wait, He's not done! The One who sat upon the throne then quickly pivoted and the next thing out of His divine mouth was this: "But I have this against you, that you have left your first love." Bing, bam, boom, bop, and roll me over with a feather! The Lord knows how to suck the air out of the room and slam the brakes on a party when He needs to!

Well, as I talk to the text, I come to the realization that the "first love" who had been left was two-fold. That's right, they left the love they first had for Christ and the love they once had for one another. Interesting. When you put it all together, you walk away with the conclusion that those folks were high and mighty with regard to the framework of "churchianity." They knew their Bible doctrine, did not tolerate stupidity from imposters, and they were poster children for what it meant to be faithful, dogged church folk! Mind you, some thirty or so years prior to that writing by John, this church was commended by Paul for their love (Ephesians 1:15–16), but now . . .

what happened? I venture to offer a really, really good answer and it's simple. What happened, I contend, was the dirty encroachment of "a casual vacancy." Indeed, what happened to them is what happens over and over again in the Christian experience, which is that we allow the slow locomotive of satanic influence to escort us to the "quicksand of the casual."

We eventually "get casual" about routinely missing out on the preached and taught Word of God. We "get casual" about our financial support of the kingdom agenda. We "get casual" about permissively allowing our eyes to feast on what will sweetly push a sin worm down our "churchified" throats. We "get casual" about our excessive use of alcohol and the utter devastation it has wrought in countless lives. We "get casual" about early indicators that our child may be poised to struggle with gender identity issues because we want to be viewed as modern. We "get casual" about soft porn. We "get casual" about not speaking up for what's right because it's easier to get along when you go along. We "get casual" about the dominance of profanity that routinely pours from our lips and its impact upon our public witness for Christ. We "get casual" about racism in the world and in the church and resist seeing it for the sin it is. We "get casual" about reminding the man or woman of God in the pastor's chair that we're standing with them and are committed to holding their hands up when they get weary. We "get casual" about sharing the gospel with co-workers because we don't want to be known as "church boy." We "get casual" about allowing our children to participate in school and community activities on Sunday mornings in place of the worship hour. We "get casual" about upholding our God-ordained sexual responsibilities (1 Corinthians 7) to our wives after being married a while which positions her to be "possibly" more vulnerable to "slick Julio," who'd be glad to "step in."

The Lord's words to the church at Ephesus should leave our knees weak. He said, "I have this against you." Let's watch out for an encroaching spiritual cancer that leaves us "casually vacant" of Holy Spirit power, conviction, depth, and leading.

Week 44

Sin Is my friend

Romans 6–7

I often feel that the good skirt-swinging and pressed suit-wearing church people aren't ready to earnestly absorb the real Paul in our text. Perhaps they prefer to sterilize and intellectualize the subterranean reality of sin, where it takes us and what it does to us. If we dare be transparent, some of us can talk in scandalous detail about our old friend, sin. When I lean into both what Paul says alongside the inferences I deduce from his intensive permutations about sin, I walk away with the clear understanding that this was a real man who wrestled with real life. If many of us could get past the pasty middle-class expression of Euro-American Christianity, we could probably better relate to the trickery of sin. Sin has mercilessly pummeled countless men as they glance down the long road that leads to full surrender. I'm talking about men with dirty underwear, foul breath, raggedy pants, shoes with holes in them crawling toward the cross where full surrender abides. But I'm also talking about clean-shaven, khaki-wearing, Armani suit-wearing, socially sophisticated, fat wallet carrying, six-figure lifelong church attenders who are likewise crawling toward the cross where full surrender awaits. Here's the thing, there are times when sin deceptively comes off as a reasonable friend and, consequently, the twisted murmurings of men often sound like this:

"It patiently waits for me, hears me out, and supports me even when wrong is upon the throne. It personally escorts brother pleasure to the door-step of my life and assassinates my occasional stupid inclination to be restricted by righteousness. It wanders the lush corner gardens of life that are lit-tered with kindness, grace, and mercy and renames them as little useless vignettes of spiritual poop. Yes, sin burrows its way into my unconscious mind and builds a link between it and the best hopes and dreams the devil has for me. It occasionally reminds me of its juicy promises and that I need not delay. Sin tells me to push my mate in the corner and require her to make me happy, even when my personal happiness means sorrow in heaven. Sin thoughtfully reminds me that I'm not here to stay, so I might as well get all that can be gotten and do it without apology. Indeed, sin says a penis isn't a penis if it's not fat with constancy and variety.

My friend, Sin, is decent enough to remind me that my intellect and masculine drives will always lead me home to my place of contentment. The thoughtfulness of my friend -Sin- frequently reminds me to focus on the weaknesses of other followers of Christ as a means to justify my own unrighteousness. Sin reminds me that if my mate fails to make me happy, there is always a "Plan B." The giving nature of sin is so wonderful that it affords me a ready-made forceful rejection against any form of Christianity that dares to require, instead of humbly request, anything of me. How can I ever thank sin for helping me realize that secular education for my kids is sacred but biblical education is entirely optional! I'm so grateful that my friend, Sin, reminds me of the truth that God has indeed failed time and time again to give me what I've asked for."

Paul urges us to walk in the newness of life and he asks the pivotal question, "Shall we continue to walk in sin and with sin and, thereby, be mastered by our old friend, Sin?" Today is a new day. Say, "Goodbye, Sin."

Week 45

Marriage Hell/Hell of a Marriage

1 Corinthians 13; Ephesians 5:21–38

Here are five direct reasons why lots of marriages can be described as "marriage hell" rather than "a hell of a marriage."

1. **Too immature**: Indeed, marriage is for real grown-ups and not for immature, self-absorbed people who happen to be of legal adult age.

2. **Too unteachable**: We all enter marriage for the first time without actual experience but when you add in one or both partners who can't be taught by anybody, or anything, watch out because hell will program its GPS for their address.

3. **Too unforgiving**: When everything that happens sticks to your emotional and psychological ribs and you have virtually no ability to allow God to take you "up and

over" or "in and thru a situation to reach resolution or acceptance," you will always live as burnt, resentful toast.

4. **Too lazy**: For sure, marriage is hard work and when one or both persons are too emotionally and mentally lazy to dig beneath a layer of dirt to find out what's at the foundation of something and too intellectually lazy to reach above low-lying clouds to ascertain better insight, it results in a suffocating, stuck-in-the-mud paralysis.

5. **Too focused on the secular rather than the sacred**: When you treat Christ and His biblical principles like pets who are only allowed in the yard and not allowed to hang out inside the house, then your house will most assuredly also be free from all that Christ and His principles have to offer.

Do you want to have a marriage from hell, or do you want to have a hell of a marriage? Remind yourself that fundamentally a man can't have a good Christian marriage if the man isn't striving to be a good Christian.

Week 46

I Don't Like Jesus

Matthew 16:23

I know it might be controversial to say but I might as well admit that I don't like the middle-class-approved crafted image of Jesus espoused by the modern church. Jesus. Religious outposts sell their specific cultural imprint of Jesus which constricts what they deem appropriate and inappropriate in worship style, clothing attire, and even approaches to evangelism. In our text, which I've alluded to before, Peter finds himself at odds with the directional intent and purpose of Jesus. Think about that because that's deeply troubling. Jesus saw the direction and purpose of His ministry one way and Peter resisted it. Said yet another way, Peter didn't like what Jesus had to say about Himself.

Consequently, Jesus took the gloves off and for his own good, gut-punched Peter to show him his error and point him to the beautiful side of the cross. That stirs a deeply uncomfortable question for me, which is this: "What realities of Christ have I been comfortably walking in misdirected denial of ?" Could it be that my stringent theology of holiness mistakenly dullens the fuller depth of compassion and patience I should have for men who are wrestling with homosexuality? If Jesus is speaking to me about this, I'll admit I'm not sure I like what Jesus has to say. Could it be that my conservative evangelical leanings cause me to be a bit narrow-minded in my judgments of Romanism and what that association signals regarding the probable or improbable acquisition of salvation? If Jesus is speaking to me about this, I'll admit I'm not sure I like what Jesus has to say. Could it be that Jesus is trying to speak to me regarding the secret condition of my heart toward certain political and religious figures whom I find abhorrent and secretly wish they'd stumble off a cliff ? Again, if Jesus is speaking to me about this, I'll admit I'm not sure I like what Jesus has to say. The Jesus we discover in the Scripture, minus the heavy overlay of ethnic, cultural, and even the political contours we sometimes forcibly imprint upon Him, was a bold, deeply substantive, forgiving, thoughtful, powerful, masculine, kindhearted, and purposeful lover of the mosaic of mankind. He was an obedient Son to the Father who seemed more comfortable with whores than fake holy men in the Temple. He was a man who was comfortable with the discomfort of truth.

I'm suspicious that if He walked among us here and now in the flesh, a lot of us Christians and "church people" would quite probably occasionally find ourselves disillusioned with Him and perplexed by Him as was Peter. Yep, in *Haynesonian* vernacular, the enigmatic Savior of the world said to his follower, Peter, "*You, sir, are full of crap.*" I love that the Savior kept it real when Peter was misaligned with the core of His identity, plan, and purpose. Like some of you, I've been around church all of my life, and on top of that, I'm a PK (preacher's kid), which means I bleed church. Admittedly, that doesn't mean that I consistently desire to understand Jesus as best I can. I do know, however, whether it is the perplexing quagmires of situational ethics or other layered diatribes of man's thinking, whatever Jesus says, will lead us to the light. I once read something that was attributed to Gandhi. While having a conversation with a Christian, Gandhi reportedly said to the Christian, " I like your Christ. I do not like your Christians. Your Christians are so unlike your Christ."[vi]

Week 47

The Humble Audacity of Me

Psalm 8; Philippians 4:9; 1 Corinthians 11:1

I often find myself partially whispering the rhetorical sentiments of the psalmist when he asked, "What is man that Thou art mindful of him?" The foundation of divinely inspired reasoning is often circular. The same man who called himself the "chief of sinners" also uttered these words, "The things you have learned and received and heard and seen in me, practice these things; and the God of peace shall be with you." Wow, that's some kind of audacity! And don't miss the intricate and detailed "check me out and do as I do" invitation to analysis. Paul is a bad, hush your mouth, let's do this kind of spiritual fighting machine! But let me quickly underscore that he was still just a man. A more comprehensive study of his life proves that he had two legs like us. He probably had a receding hairline just like us and a possible predisposition to high blood pressure, just like many of us. He had to be knocked off of his horse and have his backside thud the earth and bounce. That's right. Just like many of us, Paul had to eat dirt before God could get his attention.

Certainly, every Christian man who's not delusional knows he doesn't naturally belong in the pantheon of purity and might. Given that, it's a mind-numbing fact that the sovereign God of all creation still says to us, "Come here, because I'm about to use you!" Yeah, even though God has standards, and it's a perplexing thing at times, we must still be careful about how quickly we declare people to be "not qualified." At this point, God has not seen fit to more fully explain it to me but I have come to realize that there are instances when God will use a donkey, a whore, or a resident church ying-yang to accomplish his purposes. I admit out loud that as a preacher and leader that I'm extremely uncomfortable saying what Paul had the audacity to say regarding himself, "Follow me as I follow Christ."

Nevertheless, I understand that Paul was completely right to say it and I, too, should embrace a mentality that wisely understands the "humble audacity of me." You see, some men declare themselves not good enough.

Indeed, that is a dangerous thing to do because, in some instances, we wrongly pronounce ourselves "disqualified" when God says "qualified." In doing so, we take His authority upon ourselves and miss out on the glory of the ballooning presence of God. I cannot fully and intellectually explain God's grace and the sometimes complex triggers for God's yes, no, or not now. I can say, however, I'm exhibit number one and, despite the imperfections of me, God can still use the humble audacity of me.

Week 48

Unnecessarily Necessary?

Matthew 26; Matt 9:18–23; Romans 8:28

I wonder if you, like me, have experienced explosions you knew were God triggered and the explosions left you resentfully muttering to God, "Was that necessarily necessary?" It's true. I've encountered situations and circumstances that left me asking, "Honestly, God, why did you take it there 'cause there were definitely other options to get your point across?" I know it seems like I'm picking on Peter, and maybe I am. However, it's still true that at the defining crossroads where Jesus would either bleed to capture redemption for countless souls for all of eternity or cower in the aversion of human torture, Peter got ingloriously whacked by the Son of God publicly.

Most of us can recall advisories, warnings, foretelling rumblings, and spiritual gut checks that told us to knock off what we were doing or do what we were not doing and should be doing. The text reveals what I kinda wish it didn't reveal, which is that Peter had been warned about his impending behavior. Even yet, the itch of self-preservation oozed, leaked, and spilled out of his mouth with a denial of even knowing Jesus! All of us understand a sudden itch to do wrong, so we have the functional capacity to understand Peter although we dare not condone it.

I also understand why Jesus forewarned Peter of his impending bad behavior. Jesus was a stealthy communicator. Time and time again, throughout the gospels, we witness Jesus helping people to see Him, despite their conditions or struggles, with the expectation that seeing Him and encountering Him would help them to better see themselves and their possibilities. I'd dare to say that was a critical moment for Peter and certainly must have contributed to his impressive ministry career after the resurrection. I also can't help but think of the woman who had been bleeding for twelve long years, which was a debilitating problem in that culture and time on top of it being a health concern. While Jesus was surrounded by a crowd who had another pressing need on their minds, she managed to touch his garment. She didn't even want to be noticed but the Master paused when he saw her and His manifest power helped her see her newly healed self. Again, given the social implications of her physical condition, she undoubtedly preferred that Jesus not recognize her publicly. He decided otherwise. Likewise, Joseph, the husband of Mary, must have surely not preferred the necessary means chosen by God to usher in the Savior of the world. The coming of the long-awaited Messiah, yes, but the divine impregnation of a young lady that he was engaged to, which would be literally unbelievable to gobs of people? Joseph must have whispered a million times, "Is this necessarily necessary?"

The Word of God does not say all things are good but, rather, it says, "All things work for the good of those who love Him and are called in accordance with His purposes." My grandmother, the late Edna G. Haynes, used to often say, "Trust Him even when you can't trace Him." The prayer of my heart is, "Even when my intelligence, ideas, hidden motivations, lack of understanding, preferences, and convictions say otherwise, Lord help me to trust you even when I think your way seems unnecessarily necessary."

Week 49

I Am What I'm Not

Romans 6 and 7

I am a real man with real stereotypical hang-ups, attitudes that can be stinky, carnal leanings that want to sit in my lap, warrior drums that I beat before thinking, and a penchant for knowingly leaping from the hand of God. It is still true, however, that "I am what I'm not." With unsettling raw honesty, the Apostle Paul openly wrestled with the intersectionality of the hard realities of what and who he was in Christ over against the relentless lure to lick the often lying, sweet, and tasty "slavery of sin." I encourage you to spend some time on Romans chapters six and seven to absorb the blowing and biting wind of his real man talk and uncomfortable contemplation.

Before I crawled to a place of Christ dominance in my life, time and time again, sin lied to me. Sin told me that it could be trusted to always be truthful, but that was a lie. Sin told me that the unfolding behavioral patterns of my teen years were harmless fun, inconsequential, and disconnected to who I'd be once I hit my young adult years, but that was a lie. Sin told me that the downside of its insidious pull for me to compromise whenever it seemed advantageous for me was an upside for getting ahead in a morally vacant world, but that was a lie. Sin told me to turn down the volume on my Dad's relentless talk about personal holiness because it quite probably was not appropriately balanced with the bigness of grace, but that was a lie. In my younger years, sin told me that my public operational giftedness in ministry was so bountiful that the private thinness of my moral righteousness should be viewed as small, but that was a lie. Sin told me the discipline of Scriptural study was unnecessary at a certain point and I could simply function off the fumes of what I already knew, but that was a lie. Sin initially told me that my wife's spiritual life was her individual spiritual responsibility and mine was on me. Early on, it undercut the fact that our relationship needed to better reflect the deep connectivity of Christ's relationship to the church. So, yes, the disease-ladened tongue of sin lied to me. Sin initially told me to only live for Christ in front of my kids and that there would be no need to directly articulate the gospel, but that, too, was a lie. As I initially started my professional secular career, sin used the early indicators of professional success to signal that God would ignore the perpetual spit of offensive indiscretion, but that was a lie.

In Romans 6, Paul recognized the inescapable position of slavery. I would suggest the summation is that sin is a dirty dog and I was its slave. Sin is still a dirty dog and I'm still a slave but I am now not a slave to sin. I am a slave to righteousness and, in that way, I am what I'm not.

Week 50

When A Man Loves a Boy

Proverbs 22:6; Proverbs 17:6; Psalm 103:13;
Psalm 127:3–5

Up until about age eleven, I was raised by a woman. Yes, my mom, Susie Griffith, did all she could to lovingly teach and nurture me. However, the simple fact of the matter is that a woman cannot with full authenticity instruct a boy or be a model for a boy for what it is to be a man. Only a good man can take a boy on a high-caliber tour of manhood and more naturally prepare him for the independent solo days of manhood that are yet to come. In the 1970s, in His infinite and unanticipated mercy, God divinely spoke to time, spoke to geography, and spoke to the heart of my sister, Susie Melton. He commanded all three (time, geography, and my sister's heart) to lie across the conscientious doorstep of a real man whose name was Michael E. Haynes. Yes, a man who did not share my physical DNA, but who did bear the imprint of spiritual DNA that directed his path, heard and answered the clarion call to transcribe his love of the Father to the love of a fatherless boy. Indeed, God saw it from eternity past, ordained it, grew it, kept it, and said, "It is good."

Here's the thing. There are males of legal adult age in the body of Christ who would do well to be wise enough to go back to boy school. Yes, that's right. For many men, the trajectory of manhood is lopsided and bent. The reason is simple. The manhood prototype, which was the source of their active or passive teaching, had corrosive rot oozing thru all of their parts and particulars. In some instances, because no man could be found, the prototype was a direct pitiful invention of a boyish carnal contention of what manhood ought to look like. My only boy, Michael E. Haynes II, has fully stepped onto the stage of independent sanctified manhood. So, now that I have grown and loved a boy from boyhood to manhood, my ongoing desire has one or two possible platforms:

1. Ask God to put another fatherless boy on my pathway and grow him from boyhood to manhood.

2. Keep loving men up close and personal to help men who need assistance while journeying from legal adulthood to the domain of biblical manhood.

If God has equipped you likewise, will you also be a man who actively loves a boy or a man?

When a mature Christian man fails to love a boy or another spiritually immature man, it is not a victimless crime. The following ten things, and more, can easily happen:

1. Boys grow up clueless and don't know when, where, nor even how to properly manage their penis. Further, they have no idea or appreciation that the "sacred pleasure plumb" of a woman is directly linked to the marriage gift of Almighty God.

2. The voice of Father-God often gets drowned out by the loudness of a present but bad father or the deafening ugly silence of an absent father.

3. The church is ignored or the church and Christ are discredited because of Christian men's insensitivity in ignoring the boys.

4. A boy grows to overly identify with the power of femininity because it's what he knows best and feels most safe with.

5. Lukewarm morality adequately satisfies even though a personal relationship with the Lord God would transform and mesmerize.

6. The church has to continually stand with its hat in its hand while begging males to at least pretend to be men.

7. Future wives possibly feel weighed down by the burdensome, awkward, sippy cups their husbands rely on because their husbands were never taught manhood.

8. Teen boys run wild and undisciplined and are desperately in need of being saved from moral subjectivism.

9. Unmarried young women eventually peer into the trash cans of life, searching for anything male that might be redeemable.

10. The rightful places of men, by default, get filled by women.

Week 51

When a Man Loves a Man

1 Samuel 18; 2 Samuel 1; Romans 1

Alfred W. Jones was the first male friend I came to love with full self-awareness of my deep and abiding love for another male. We didn't attend the same elementary school but my best recollection is that I was in the sixth grade when we met at church. I would contend that a man who is continuously absent from the benefit of a deep and abiding male friendship dwells in a certain state of abject relational poverty. Although my connectivity with Alfred Jones has experienced varying degrees of active connectivity for approximately fifty years, the knowledge that he's there can be likened to a faithful old oak that stays put no matter the many places I've traveled. No matter the entrance and exits of other friendships, no matter what calm or turbulence life hurls in my direction, Alfred has always been there and my bet is that he would say the same about me.

The friendship between David and Jonathan is legendary and well worth real-life contemplation, so I hope you'll take some time to visit or revisit their friendship journey. Needless to say, the world almost always seeks to pollute and bend anything pure and straight. So it has, of course, tried to suggest that a homoerotic thread flowed beneath David and Jonathan's relationship but there is nothing to support that perversion. Often, before a deep and abiding friendship between men can be established, father time needs to hang around for a while but the text signals that David and Jonathan took a strong shine toward one another quickly. As men, we have a long history of fighting over women. We allow women to cause male friendship diminishments and the rejection of outstretched male hands of counsel because we're made drunk by the tender bosoms of women. We dismiss other men who don't measure up to our prescribed cultural or sub-cultural views of what masculinity looks like.

There are multiple observational nuggets that David and Jonathan's friendship offers but I'll offer just a few that immediately capture my attention.

First: Eat, Swallow, Digest, and Expel the Expressive Pill of Tenderness. Both at the front and the back of their relationship, there can be found a shameless annunciation of love. At the outset of their relationship, Jonathan pledged a covenantal relationship with David. Although he was the King's son, he took off his own robe and placed it on his new bestie, David! After King Saul and Jonathan died in ugly deaths in battle, David unabashedly poured out his heart regarding his beloved homeboy, Jonathan. He said, "I am distressed for you, my brother Johnathan. You have been very pleasant to me and your love to me was more wonderful than the love of women." Wow, David, are you serious? Let's remind ourselves that very few men of record did more female taste testing than David. Yet, his deep and abiding friendship with Jonathan apparently knitted something in his heart and soul that even exceeded the dizzying and bountiful interlockings with women. Admittedly, at that still relatively early stage in his life, we don't know what David had been up to but, if his future exploits were at all reflective of his unknown youthful urgings, that was a man who fully understood the weight of his declaration. Guys, let's reach for the often elusive expressions of affection in our close bromances and, yeah, let's even dare to be as transparent about our man-on-man love as was David and Jonathan.

Second: Don't Let the Stench of Stinky Family Ties Stop You. Jonathan was King Saul's son and King Saul quickly became a massive, hate your guts, wanna kill you twice enemy to David. Yet, David continued to open his heart to the King's kid, Jonathan. That is an uncomfortable example for me because there have been many times that I've declined a friendship solely based upon who was in that person's family and I was wrong. Men, if God calls us to a friendship, let's trust God to protect us in the friendship despite who the person may be connected to. It's also worth underscoring that all friendships require some degree of risks and, although you may, in fact, incur some cuts and bruises, if God called you to it, He can empower you to survive it. Friendship possibilities can include those not part of our long-held political affiliations. They can also include those sullied by past criminal activity or people of different ethnic, cultural, and religious backgrounds. Let me throw this in as well— let's not miss the valuable specter of friendship that can be lost when we're overly concrete about who is and who is not our approximate socio-economic equal. That can cause us to wrongly judge another man's intrinsic value, and that dumb error can, of course, flow in both socio-economic directions.

Third: Live in Friendships Before You Die. The sad thing for me is that Jonathan died an early death, relatively speaking. That's right, he met David at the front side of David becoming known because David had successfully taken on Goliath and the Philistines. He then lived through the fifteen or so years that his father pursued David in an attempt to kill him, but he died alongside his father and never got to see his friend succeed his father and become King. Men, since none of us know when we will die or when others will die, let's seize the opportunity now as it relates to bonding in close male friendships that God brings to the pathway of our lives. By the way, David extended his heart of friendship to Jonathan even after Jonathan was dead, and in that way, he kept the friendship alive. How? David tangibly reached out to meaningfully support Jonathan's son, Mephibosheth. Yes, it's a beautiful thing when a man loves a man.

Week 52

Nuggets From the Door Knock of Death

Genesis 49 & 50; 1 Kings 2:1–12; 2 Kings 2:2;
Timothy 4; Genesis 24–25

My Dad often used to say, "You'll see the best and worst of humanity at weddings and at funerals." On September 12, 2019, God allowed death to issue a summons to my Dad. I, along with other family members, held a vigil at his bedside as that great man of God transitioned to the other side of eternity. As some will do even in the cave of their individualized grieving process, I sought to ask, "What new insight is to be known or relearned inside my cave of dire loss?" Frankly, I don't think I have arrived at complete answers to the question but here are some nuggets that I hope will benefit other real men who already have had to, or will need to someday, navigate the death of a positive and impactful father.

These nuggets emanate from the daddy death experiences of two Old Testament men, Joseph and Elisha (Genesis 49 & 50, 2 Kings 2).

Joseph: The entire life of Joseph is riddled with declarations of a familial mess, percolating sexual landmines, soaring spiritual grit, signals of homage to ancestral foundations, and high descendant expectations. In Joseph's later years, the closing chapter of his father's life, Jacob, was littered with multiple transformative moments. Here are just a few nuggets of learning that roll off the deck of Joseph's life when the knock of death stepped to his dad's front door.

First, if you have the benefit of smelling death's approaching scent at your dad's door, and your dad has some things to say, be sure to shut up and listen. Knowing his departure was near, Jacob gathered Joseph and his brothers around his death bed and to say he left them speechless is an understatement because of the way he spoke of their future. Alongside Jacob's prophetic profundity was the beautiful gift Joseph and his brothers gave their father which was open ears and shut mouths. If

I can briefly dot around the Scriptures, a quick scriptural glance at fatherly words and behavior toward the end of Paul's life underscores the importance of such moments. Somehow, Paul sniffed out the encroachment of death. His closing admonishments to his son in the ministry, Timothy, were punctuated with wise counsel regarding Timothy's responsibility to be a trumpet of truth. Likewise, as Abraham knowingly closed the curtain of life, he was strategic in how he used the customs of the day to make sure a godly woman was at Isaac's side. David's closing counsels of life for his son, Solomon, are rich, meaty morsels and perhaps reflective of all he had learned from both his life victories and defeats. So, yes, guys, if death's day for dad still hangs out in the future and you have the advantage of sensing its nearing, be sure to absorb all thoughts that a wise and godly father may have to share, verbally and/or behaviorally.

Second, I love that Joseph and his brothers sought to honor their dad in death by going out of their way sacrificially showing care for what was important to him. He wanted to be buried at his chosen gravesite in Israel and not in Egypt, where they were living. Much is dictated by the practical realities of what's convenient and inconvenient in our modern context because we live busy lives. Men, if you know what your dad wants and you're able to make it happen, step up and make it happen. I'm speaking here both from what I implicitly see in the texts as well as personal experience. There was something my dad desired of me, he verbalized it, and I did it. There was also something he didn't verbalize, but I nevertheless knew he desired it and I didn't do it. I'll always regret not doing it.

Third, while Joseph and his brothers all had adult lives, including wives, children, and other responsibilities, the importance of the loss was reflected in how much time was made to yield appropriate tributes to a dad who had sacrificed so much. As you read through the text, take note of the intricate ceremonial steps and the requirement of time. For us, most assuredly, the many pulls and pushes in modern-day living should be made to bend and bow to the necessary time that's needed to pay tribute to an impactful father.

Fourth, with the shadow of death nearby, don't miss how emotionally ripped Joseph was when his brothers revealed their fear that their dad's death might mean Joseph was about to get revenge for the wrongs that were done to him earlier in life. Let's all learn from his example and not let the yuck of family hurt, unhealthy behavior, perceived wrongs, or flat-out past putrid assaults further propel our families into the abyss of dysfunction. While the function of repentance has its appropriate place inside family dynamics, let's still commit, like Joseph, to acting as a soothing salve on exposed wounds. For sure, like Joseph, do not raise your hand metaphorically speaking or otherwise to further exact injury.

Elisha: I particularly love Elisha's journey because he got to walk in the sweet shadow of Elijah's armpit. Elijah didn't produce Elisha by physical birth but he poured into him his life like any father would who has a much-beloved son. Here are a few real man nuggets to take note of as the scent of Elijah's departure from this life was imminent.

First, similarly to Joseph and his brothers, notice that Elisha stubbornly gave his dad/mentor the gift of presence. Be it Bethel, Jericho, or Jordan, Elisha had the benefit of being privy to a life's clock that was winding down and he stubbornly refused to leave Elijah's side. Unlike prior eras, we live in a time when families have often spread out from one another, so giving the gift of presence becomes quite tricky. Nevertheless, Elisha's behavior shoves me in a corner, sticks a finger in my face, and whispers to my spirit, "There are times when a man has to just do it."

Second, don't quickly run by the implications of Elisha's request to Elijah to pass on to him a double portion. You see, it's important to not romanticize Elijah's life because he was indeed a tough and real man who knew what it was to be a fugitive on the run from a bloodthirsty and powerful queen who wanted to gut him like a fish. He knew what it was to sit in his own filth and funk while licking his emotional wounds from loneliness and exhaustion. He knew what it was to stand in a crowd and dare to rely on God to produce an unlikely miracle. He knew what it was to have a growling physical belly even while divine power coursed through his frail body. So, while he had been a witness to amazing things, it's still true that he spent a lot of time in good trouble. It is significant that Elisha dared to ask for a double portion because it was tantamount to asking for double trouble! Men, like Elisha, we also need to stand where we need to be to get what we need to have, no matter the costs!

Third, don't miss the quickness of behavioral execution by Elisha once Elijah had been taken from this valley of tears. Immediately, we see Elisha back at the Jordan where he had previously witnessed Elijah slap the water with his mantle and the Jordan parted so they could walk on dry ground. I love that he took the mantle that had been left for him and that he went back to the place that was between him and the Jordan and had enough faith to exercise the authority that had been passed to him by God. He dared to walk in Elijah's footsteps and began immediately executing signals of spiritual greatness.

Week 53

Be Alive When You Die

Deuteronomy 31–34

I don't know why but I remember being nine years old. It probably has something to do with the chocolate brown suit in my closet that made me feel, without a doubt, how good I looked wearing it. It's a little unsettling at times for me to acknowledge that I now have more of the road of life behind me than in front of me. I thank God for my dad for multiple reasons. One of the things I'm thankful for is that he allowed me a front-row seat to his aging process and, yes, his journey to the closing shades of life. On that journey, I was mostly a quiet listener. I absorbed the inglorious twists and turns of failing health, diminishing mental acuity, and also the creeping reality of growing dependence upon others. As my dad taught me to do, I often found myself nestled between the pages of Holy writ as I sought, and still seek, solace in the numbing realization that God closed his life even though he was still so alive before he had to die.

I can't say how many times I've quietly read through the broader contextual chapters that recount the impending death of Moses. On one occasion, with the loss of my dad rumbling around in my heart, I consciously saw some connective tissue between Moses and my dad that hadn't occurred to me before. I'm holding on to the modeling I see in these two great men because they are good nuggets for all men. Especially men who've arrived at the stage where they have to work exponentially harder to maintain muscle mass, keep an eye on prostate issues, and often can't find stuff that's right in front of them. I have often said, "If you talk to the text, the text will talk back to you." So, the waning days and hours of the life of Moses is a good place to take a seat and watch how a real man can die well. I start each of the five nuggets below by referencing the fact that Moses did have mess-ups. I want to keep in view that the valiant close to the life that wonderfully included God serving as the private undertaker for Moses did not mean he was a man who did not have mess-ups. That is a simple but important truth because many of us will someday step to the doorstep of death quickly or progressively with the waving hand of regrettable mess-ups in our rearview mirror. Still, that truth can never cancel the shores of greatness that God desires our feet to tread upon before life closes. Greatness is not defined by your name being up in lights somewhere but, rather, it's more akin to you becoming a friend of God.

1. **While Moses did not live a mess-up-free life, at the close of his days, he was still a man with whom God chose to have conversations.** Sometimes, as Christian men age, regressive dullness sets in spiritually when progressive sharpness is needed to bolster our "old warrior" status. Have you ever received a defining communicative outreach that spoke volumes to you about how the person felt about you? I'm struck by how God saw value in talking to Moses right up to the end of his life and how Moses had wax-free ears that heard and obeyed God. Let's strive to be aging men who talk to God and who God desires to talk with.

2. **While Moses did not live a mess–up–free life, at the close of his days, he still had some ministry snap, crackle, and pop and people knew when he spoke that it was a God moment.** In my sanctified imagination, I can see the wilderness nation gathered shoulder to shoulder in stark silence to hear Moses relay to them what God had spoken to him. To march toward the close of life with that kind of impactful tongue presupposes that a man has learned God and life in a way that shows others that he's become an uncommon friend of God. At least three times toward the closing period of the life of Moses, I'm awestruck by the words in the text, "So, Moses went and spoke these words to all Israel. And he said to them, the Lord has said to me." (Deuteronomy 31:1–2). Again, he spoke a song in the hearing of the assembly. "Give ear, O heavens, and let me speak; and let the earth hear the words of my mouth." And yes, "Let my teaching drop as the rain." (Deuteronomy 3:21–2) Men, it's both important what you say about God and what God says about you. At the end of his life, God's

behavior says something really powerful about what God had to say about Moses. One of the significant consequences of the bidirectional communication between Moses and God was that the people of God were further positioned to achieve their destiny. For those of a certain age who naturally think about the shorter road that lies ahead, let's again determine to live before God and with others with some spiritual snap, crackle, and pop.

3. **While Moses did not live a mess–up–free life, at the close of his days, there is not even a hint of a propensity to hug the kiss of possible compromise.** "Nope, I ain't gonna do it your way." Those are the words that our behavior often speak to the known will of God as we deal with different situations in our lives. Follow Moses toward the close of his life and there isn't even a hint of stubbornness or a refusal to do things God's way. Men, many of us age and become like old goats who refuse to eat fresh messaging from God because a long time ago, he started us out eating

certain greenery from a certain place. It doesn't occur to us that God could be trying to reroute our pathway in a way that leads to a new pasture location. From man's rationale, it would have been understandable if Moses had attempted to subvert God's announced plans. After all, on the surface of things, arguably, it made no sense to put the nation's leader in a private graveyard just at the hour the people were being called upon to seize land that had been in their sight for forty years! Like Moses, however, let's reach for stubborn obedience that swallows the will of God, whole. That includes an apparent summons that sidelines us from what we might feel we have a right to be directly involved with or something we have no desire to be involved with, even though God says to do it.

4. **While Moses did not live a mess–up–free life, at the close of his days, I'm imprinted by the scent of tenderness as he spoke to the nation, including sharing a sweet song that spoke to slices of their history and God's care.** As the author of the Pentateuch, Moses acts as a God–

directed author and archivist. Time and again, we are witnesses to his deliberate investiture and thereby preservation of information that spoke to who God was, what He'd done, and what He required. May it likewise be true that our tongues can be used to speak a word of witness to the movement of God in our families, in our communities, our world, and, yes, in our individual lives. When you open your mouth and say what you're supposed to say, when you're supposed to say it, and to whom you're supposed to say it, it means that generations to come will likely be the beneficiaries of a verbal or written record of the exploits of our mighty God.

5. **While Moses did not live a mess–up–free life**, **he was still resigned to the sovereignty of God**, **who told him, "It's time to die."** Many of us have been around long enough to witness folk near the brink of death but still voicing displeasure about its proximity. As a pastor, I've long been intrigued by the apparent behavioral contradiction to our declared theology. We teach about the wonders of

heaven and we even sing thunderously about its anticipated glory. In over forty years of ministry, I've only occasionally witnessed an apparent death march by individuals who were peacock pleased to be close to the point of seeing the God of heaven and earth. Lean in and watch Moses carefully. He accepted death, not because he was sick of being old and tired, but rather because God had spoken and said it was to be so. Obviously, how we live is of critical importance, but might I suggest that Moses also taught us something about dying.

The late Nathaniel Niles was a politician, lawyer, judge, poet, and songwriter. In the late 1800s, while sitting on a railway car on his way to work, he penned the glorious hymn in the margins of a newspaper entitled, "Precious Promise (I Will Guide Thee)." Again, most especially if you're a man of a certain age, let the below stanzas from that great hymn of the church take up residence in your soul and be akin to how you desire to die.

" *When thy secret hopes have perished, in the grave of years gone by, let this promise still be cherished, I will guide thee with Mine eye.*
When the shades of life are falling, and the hour has come to die, hear thy trusty Pilot calling, I will guide thee with Mine eye. "[vii]

It's a scandalous pitiful shame that some Christian men live as if they are dead before they die. So, let's commit to being fully spiritually alive at whatever time we die.

Author

Rev. Dr. Randy M. Haynes is a native son of Greenville, Mississippi. Having relocated to Boston, Massachusetts early in life, he graduated from the Boston Public Schools. Subsequently, he earned a BA in Theology, a Master's degree in Ministry, and a Doctorate in Ministry. He is the son of the late Rev. Dr. Michael E. Haynes, who was Boston's Dean of the Clergy and longtime Pastor of the historic Twelfth Baptist Church of Boston.

Pastor Haynes has served with distinction for years in ministry leadership over a broad spectrum, including children and youth, young adults, choral music, senior adults, and biblical education. With forty years of ministerial experience, Pastor Haynes has become known as an exceptional teacher and preacher. After moving to Virginia in 2006, he became the founding Pastor of an exciting church plant known as *Open the Book Ministries, Inc.* Having retired as the senior pastor, he now serves as the Overseer of that ministry which is now known as *The Word Church of Virginia.* Additionally, Pastor Haynes served as a Teaching Pastor at Christian Fellowship Church in Ashburn, Virginia and as a Consultant for NorthStar Church Network in Northern Virginia.

Before full-time ministry, Pastor Haynes had a distinguished career as a criminal justice official, which included an appointment as a Chief of Probation for the Massachusetts Trial Court. Pastor Haynes was a frequent lecturer at colleges and universities throughout New England as a recognized authority on juvenile delinquency, substance abuse and treatment, and community policing. He also served on Curry College's faculty in Milton, Massachusetts as an adjunct professor and taught criminal justice courses in the sociology department. Having served on multiple social, welfare, and criminal justice agencies and boards, Pastor Haynes sought to uplift poor and disenfranchised people in the community where he came of age.

For thirty-three years, Pastor Haynes has been married to a dynamic woman of God, Lisa J. Haynes, and they are the parents of eight adult children and a growing tribe of grandchildren.

References

[i] Miriam-Webster.com

[ii] YouVersion The Bible App, version 8.16.4, New American Standard

[iii] Dr. Charles Swindoll, Nothing New, July 3, 2020

[iv] Dr. Martin Luther King Speech, I Have A Dream, April 23, 1963

[v] Citizenship in a Republic; Theodore Roosevelt, Man in the Arena; April 23, 1910; p. 7.

[vi] The Christ of the Indian Road by E. Stanley Jones, Kessinger Publishing, 2005

[vii] Precious Promise; Nathaniel Niles, 1871